THE ARCHITECTURE OF OTTOMAN JERUSALEM

AN INTRODUCTION

Robert Hillenbrand

For the Muslims of the Old City of Jerusalem

THE ARCHITECTURE OF OTTOMAN JERUSALEM

AN INTRODUCTION

Robert Hillenbrand

ALTAJIR WORLD OF ISLAM TRUST

First published 2002
by
Altajir World of Islam Trust
11 Elvaston Place London SW7 5QG
Tel: 020 7581 3522
Fax: 020 7584 1977

ISBN 1 901435 09 1

Cover illustration: the (essentially) Ottoman Holy City, taken before the aesthetic and integrated balance of the skyline was marred by high-rise buildings in the second half of the 20th century. *(Photograph © Alistair Duncan)*

Front cover calligraphy by 'Nassar'

Edited by Leonard Harrow
Produced by Fox Communications and Publications, London E18 2PW
Printed in England by the St Edmundsbury Press

PUBLISHER'S PREFACE

It was a privilege for the Altajir World of Islam Trust to publish in November 2000 *Ottoman Jerusalem: The Living City 1517-1917* (edited by Sylvia Auld and Robert Hillenbrand), a major study of an historic period of one of this planet's spiritual epicentres.

From all over the world many people of different faiths come to Jerusalem to seek enlightenment and understanding of the role played down the centuries by this Holy City. This small book is designed to be a 'pocket companion' for such visitors, particularly those who are also interested in her architecture.

Robert Hillenbrand has studied and written on Islamic art and architecture for many years and we are delighted to publish herein his thoughts and observations on the architecture of Ottoman Jerusalem.

Also included within these covers is a list of the contributing authors in the main (two-part) publication, which we hope will encourage those who wish to delve further into this fascinating subject.

Alistair Charteris Duncan
Director, Altajir World of Islam Trust
London, October 2001

Robert Hillenbrand is Professor of Islamic Art at the University of Edinburgh

CONTENTS

FOREWORD

The prime purpose of this book is to provide a concise and easily usable introduction to the buildings of Ottoman Jerusalem, principally those of the 16th and 17th centuries when building activity was at its height, and to sketch their historical, religious and social context. If it finds its way into the hands of visitors to the Old City and helps them to understand better what they see, I shall be well satisfied. It is intended also to cast some light on a rather neglected corner of Islamic architecture, poised somewhat uncomfortably between the major cities of the Near East and between the medieval and modern periods. It is based on a long acquaintance with the buildings it describes, but it is also a very much expanded version (double the length, in fact) of a chapter which I contributed to *Ottoman Jerusalem, The Living City 1517-1917*, which I co-edited with Sylvia Auld (2 parts, 1,168 pages, Altajir World of Islam Trust, London, 2000). That is now the place to look for further details on the manifold problems raised by these buildings. The fact that I have been able to broaden and deepen my earlier overview is in no small measure due to the scholarly quality of many of the contributions to that massive work. In particular, I would single out my debt to Muhammad al-'Alami, Mahmud Atallah, Sylvia Auld, Michael Burgoyne, Michael Meinecke (though he was not, in fact, a contributor to that work), David Myres, Yusuf Natsheh, Abdul-Karim Rafeq and Khadr Salameh; I have profited substantially from their expertise, most particularly from that of Dr Natsheh, and can only hope that I have put it to proper use. The deliberately limited scope of this book, and its primary purpose as an introduction to the architecture of Ottoman Jerusalem, has led me to dispense with footnotes, but most of the contributions of these scholars to my text can be traced in the parent publication. I should emphasise, too, that the absence of detailed discussion of the Dome of the Rock, one of the jewels in the crown of Ottoman Jerusalem, is no accidental oversight. I am currently preparing a detailed study of the building and its post-Umayyad afterlife, and my hope is that its Ottoman history will fall into place in that wider context.

In addition to the scholarly debts noted above, I would like to express my deep gratitude to Dr Sylvia Auld, who proved a fount of wisdom, information, ideas and inspiration at every turn in the preparation of this book, whose text she read carefully. Her extensive knowledge of Jerusalem, built up over more than three decades, which she shared so generously with me and which is nourished by her deep personal commitment to the city and its people, was absolutely indispensable. My warm thanks go also to Martin Dow for much useful information on vernacular architecture in the city, and to Dr Yusuf Natsheh for his kindness in showing me around the Ottoman buildings to which he has devoted so much of his life.

I am particularly grateful to the British School of Archaeology in Jerusalem and its officers and staff for many a warm welcome to the city over the last quarter of a century, and to the staff of the Administration of Auqaf and Islamic Affairs, Jerusalem, and its Department of Islamic Archaeology, for friendly help and guidance in the course of my many visits. As always, I am beholden to Alistair Duncan (Director, Altajir World of Islam Trust) whose vision and amiable importunity persuaded me, in the teeth of other pressing obligations, to undertake this labour of love.

Robert Hillenbrand
Edinburgh, October 2001

1   INTRODUCTION

The particular importance of the architecture of Ottoman Jerusalem does not, paradoxically enough, lie in its intrinsically high quality. Instead, it is significant for a variety of quite different reasons. One is the way that the public architecture of the Ottoman centuries in Jerusalem was almost unswervingly dedicated to religious purposes. This was not a matter of course. It was very far from being the case in other Near Eastern cities like Hama, Damascus and Aleppo. In all these towns secular buildings abounded in Ottoman times. Many of the individual buildings of Ottoman public architecture in Jerusalem may be somewhat undistinguished. But, taken all together, that architecture makes a powerful cumulative impact as the physical record of centuries of unpretentious devotion to the Holy City and to the Muslim religious life practised there, in the shadow of the great charismatic monuments which dominate the Haram. In particular, the clustering of the Ottoman buildings in the Haram helps to make

them more than the sum of their parts.

Another reason why this architecture is significant is again paradoxical, namely the modest scale of practically all of these buildings. Here the contrast with the immediately preceding Mamluk period is indeed striking. In Ottoman times the absence of large mosques, capacious *madrasas* or *ribats*, urban palaces, mausolea or caravansarais is quite remarkable. Yet the patrons of the 16th and 17th centuries were undoubtedly, as in Mamluk times, members of the contemporary élite. Clearly the fashion was for unobtrusive buildings that catered either for the population at large—*sabils*, prayer platforms, open-air *mihrabs*—or, in the case of the *khalwas*, for small groups, often those that shared some specific affiliation: Sufis, perhaps, or pilgrims from Africa. These Ottoman religious buildings make their own distinctive contribution to the reassuringly human scale of the Old City as the visitor experiences it to this day.

1 A view of Jerusalem (*c.* 1895) looking west from the Wadi Jauz (Père Savignac, Collection of École Biblique).

A third reason for the importance of the Ottoman architectural heritage in Jerusalem follows directly from this, namely the evidence it presents as to the physical character of a pre-modern Islamic city which was a goal of pilgrimage. There are many such cities scattered throughout the Islamic world—Mulay Idris in Morocco, Qairawan in Tunisia, Najaf and Karbala in Iraq, Qum and Mashhad in Iran, Mazar-i Sharif in Afghanistan—and the list could be lengthened indefinitely. Not one of them is so much of a piece as an authentic pre-modern urban entity as is the Old City of Jerusalem. And that is an Ottoman achievement. Even today, when the fabric of the Old City is under such severe and unremitting strain from political, economic and demographic pressures, all of them tending towards breakneck modernisation and the destruction of cultural heritage, it has somehow managed to retain—against all the odds—its physical integrity. It simply works as a traditional Middle Eastern city long accustomed to welcoming visitors and pilgrims. The fabric of that living entity is—it is worth repeating—largely Ottoman. In that respect, it reflects the reality that *c.* 1500 and *c.* 1800—i.e. before the onset of the modern age and the exponential increase in the city's population—this was an overwhelmiingly Muslim tow, as indeed the *sijill*s confirm. The Ottomans built it to last, and it has indeed lasted superlatively well.

Finally, these buildings as a group matter because, to a degree unparalleled in any comparably large and varied group of 16th-17th-century monuments in the Islamic world, they are contextualised by written sources. These sources, the registers (*sijill*s) of the Shari'a Court in Jerusalem, are a veritable treasure trove of information. They reveal who built these monuments and why, what materials were used and how much they cost, how much the builders and labourers (skilled and unskilled) were paid, how complaints about the use of the buildings were presented and dealt with and what the legal procedures were for repairs and demolition. They detail the conditions and provisions of instruments of endowment *(waqf)*, how the

2 **An example of the script encountered in the Jerusalem *Sijill*s (Sijill 1A, 299-300)**

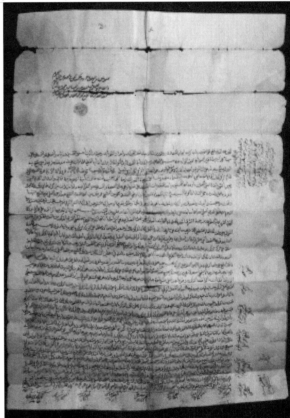

3 **An original *waqf* document dating to 1136/1724**

buildings functioned from day to day and how changes of function, staff and use occurred, and a host of other details. In comparison with Western Europe the Islamic world is relatively poor in archives more than a couple of centuries old, and as a result the information base for the researcher is somewhat limited. Not in Jerusalem. The degree to which the authorities watched over the city's buildings and protected the rights of minorities and disadvantaged is eye-opening. All this is meat and drink to the social historian, while for the architectural historian it is a fascinating exercise to trace the fortunes of a single building over several centuries—a salutary reminder that buildings are organic, that they often have a busy afterlife, and that they must not be treated as if they had been deep-frozen on the day of their completion.

These various reasons, then, should help to explain why the architecture of Ottoman Jerusalem constitutes a case study of absorbing interest to scholars—and to all lovers of that unique city—on several quite distinct counts. It is now time to investigate the context of that architecture in greater detail.

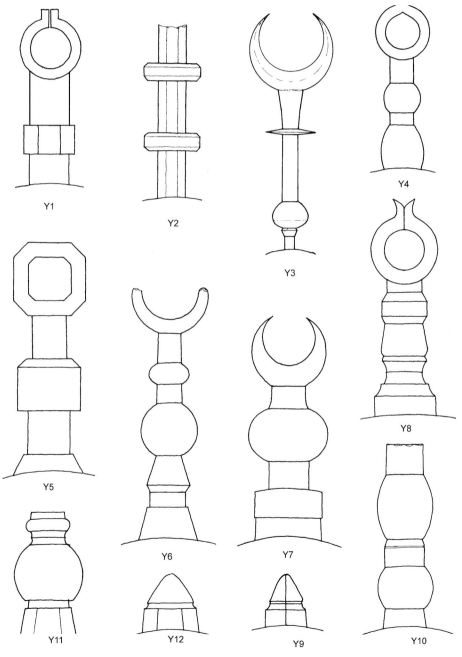

4 Finials

2 FROM MAMLUKS TO OTTOMANS: HISTORY AND HERITAGE

2.1 The historical setting

In 1453 Mehmed the Conqueror had fulfilled the long-term Ottoman ambition to capture Constantinople and to take over the territories of Byzantium. But his successors, not content with this, had sought to extend Ottoman power to the south, which resulted in their conquest of the Levant and Egypt, and—almost simultaneously— to the east. They had thus become embroiled in long-running, inconclusive and costly hostilities with Iran. Not content with this, Sulaiman the Magnificent had embarked on a series of imperial campaigns (ten in all) in eastern and south-eastern Europe. Thus by 1536, when—some twenty years after their conquest of Jerusalem—the Ottoman authorities began their first projects of serious architectural patronage in the city, their empire was firmly committed to a war on two fronts, both of them far from the Levant. The intensification of Ottoman interest in the European and Iranian theatres of war could not fail to give Sulaiman, as the Ottoman sultan, a perspective on Jerusalem which differed radically from that of his Mamluk predecessors—although, like them, he saw himself as the leader of the Sunni Muslim world, which gave an extra edge to his conflict with Shi'ite Iran. For the Mamluks, Jerusalem was centrally placed in an empire which stretched the full length of the Levantine seaboard and also encompassed Egypt and Western Arabia. Moreover, it was they who had definitively liberated the Holy Land from Frankish hands and who had thus set the seal on a campaign of *jihad* inaugurated in the early 12th century and fostered by such legendary Ayyubid and Mamluk rulers as Zengi, Nur al-Din, Saladin and Baibars. Just as the Crusaders had celebrated their capture of Jerusalem with a building boom there, so too did the Mamluks inaugurate a comparable boom when they took over control of the city. They had fought hard for Jerusalem and it had a special place in their affections. There was no reason for the Ottomans to share this view, though it is worth noting that they too had their building boom in the decades following their own capture of the city. Much the same happened after the Ottoman conquest of Baghdad in 1534: Sulaiman ordered a dome built over the tomb of Abu Hanifa and restored the tomb of 'Abd al-Qadir al-Jilani, the founder of the Qadiriyya *tariqa*. Seen in this historical perspective, it is hard not to view these successive outbursts of intensive architectural construction as a way of signalling the transfer of both cities to new masters. But it was Sulaiman's work in Jerusalem that was destined to have the more permanent impact. Both the Mamluk and the Ottoman dynasties were of course of Turkish blood, but the critical difference was that the Mamluk capital at Cairo, the major city of the arabophone world, put Jerusalem in a key position in a fundamentally Arab context. It was within easy range of Cairo, and had the further advantage of being located on one of the roads between Cairo and the other two major Mamluk cities of Damascus and Aleppo. Conversely the removal of the capital from Cairo to Istanbul doomed Jerusalem.

The Ottomans, like the Mamluks, maintained the useful fiction of allegiance to a puppet caliph, and as self-styled rulers of the orthodox Muslim world they took over the guardianship of the Holy Places, which naturally

5 Dome of the Rock, detail of a tile panel on the western façade

2.2 The differences between Ottoman and Mamluk Jerusalem

The differences between Ottoman and Mamluk architecture in Jerusalem are diagnostic of a sea-change in the role of the city. From a religious point of view, very little had changed, at least outwardly; the Ottomans, as noted above, took over from the Mamluks the self-styled office of Guardian of the Holy Places, and like them embellished Mecca, Madina and Jerusalem. But the nature of their patronage in Jerusalem was very different, as will be discussed in Chapter 6 below. Its most spectacular expression was two-fold. One element was the refurbishment of the Dome of the Rock, which appears quite simply to have been unnecessary since there is no evidence that the Umayyad external mosaics which rendered the building unique had suffered serious damage over the centuries. Thus to modern eyes the Ottomans seem to have destroyed something exceptional in order to replace it by something commonplace—at least in the Iranian world, where glazed tilework in various forms had been the preferred medium for external decoration for well over two centuries. Moreover, the signature of a Persian master from Tabriz, a certain 'Abdallah, in the tympanum above the outer north door of the Dome of the Rock testifies to a Persian presence in this ambitious scheme of re-tiling. On the other hand, there is no obvious parallel in the earlier architecture of the Ottoman lands for external tilework on this scale and quality. In Ottoman terms, then, this was a striking innovation. Perhaps the closest parallel, the Çinili Köşk in Istanbul—traditionally attributed to a Persian architect, Kamal al-Din, and following a Persian model as well—dates from almost a century earlier (1472) and remains essentially a stone monument, with tilework restricted to a highlighting function. Some 15th-century Ottoman buildings at Bursa also experiment with

included Jerusalem as the site of the First *Qibla*. But they did so from a very different geopolitical stance. Their pressing interests lay to the north-west and to the east, not in the Levant. For them, Syria, Palestine, Egypt and Arabia were provinces of a much larger empire whose centre of gravity lay in Anatolia and the Balkans. These provinces were a source of revenue, manpower and raw materials; otherwise they were of secondary interest. They were governed by appointees from Istanbul, where the metropolitan court and administration were Turkish in speech and largely Persian in culture. The relatively modest scale of Ottoman architectural patronage in Jerusalem makes sense only in the context of this seismic shift in geopolitical, linguistic and cultural realities. Stripped of its special status under the Mamluks, reduced to the role of a minor provincial town, ruled by Muslims who—however sympathetic they were to Arab culture—nevertheless owed their first loyalty to the Turkish sultan in distant Istanbul, Jerusalem under the Ottomans had definitively relinquished its position at centre stage. The architecture built there by the Ottoman authorities inevitably betrays this dramatic change in its role. It is this context that best explains the unprecedented emphasis on repair work rather than spectacular brand-new buildings in the Ottoman contribution to the architecture of the city.

external tilework, and use that medium even more lavishly for their interiors. Thereafter, interest in this type of ornament waned among Ottoman architects until the middle of the 16th century, with the refurbishing of the Dome of the Rock. This may itself have been the reviving factor. But, with a few exceptions—notably the sumptuously, perhaps even excessively, decorated interior of the Rüstem Pasha mosque (*c.* 1561), the mosque of Ramazan Effendi (1585-6) and the Takkeci Ibrahim Çavuş (1592)—tilework was confined to key locations rather than in overall fashion. To that extent, then, the exterior tilework of the Dome of the Rock is as exceptional in an Ottoman context as it is typical of a Persian one.

The work of Sulaiman the Magnificent could therefore be seen as an attempt to stake a claim to this especially holy site, and to ottomanise its appearance in an unmistakable way—for glazed tilework could not fail to have been recognised at the time as a foreign kind of decoration in the local context. Significantly, the interior, which naturally lacked the exceptional visibility, and therefore the propaganda potential, of the exterior, was left virtually untouched. The second element of Ottoman patronage was the walls, including the Citadel (probably 938/1531-2). Here, too, the political statement is unmistakable (see Chapter 3 below). The third most holy city of Islam, which had remained without continuous walls, and therefore obviously vulnerable, since Ayyubid times, was now fully protected—this was the long arm of the Ottoman sultan in action. As in the case of the Dome of the Rock, the visual impact was what mattered. Hence, perhaps, the warlike battlements, more for show than use. Much of the new walling was too low and too frail to offer serious protection against a determined enemy or artillery bombardment. Happily the city was not called upon to endure such tests.

These, then, were the two most public expressions of Ottoman patronage, and there can be little doubt that they had an incomparably greater impact on the local population, and on

visitors and pilgrims—always an important category in Jerusalem—than any two Mamluk foundations in the city. But, with the single exception of Khassaki Sultan, the rest of the Ottoman buildings reveal a very modest financial commitment to the city's architecture on the part of the Ottoman regime and its functionaries. Their rule lasted almost twice as long as that of the Mamluks, and yet it produced only a fraction of the Mamluk output in terms of quality and scale of buildings. True, there are plenty of them; but as a group they are undistinguished. What is the explanation?

The basic factor seems to be geopolitical. For the Mamluks, ensconced in Egypt with important provincial capitals in Damascus and Aleppo, Jerusalem was relatively close to the centres of power. It straddled the route to Syria. It therefore had strategic as well as religious importance and was an integral part of a relatively small and self-contained state. With the Ottoman conquest, all this changed. The new masters of Jerusalem had much wider horizons than the Mamluks had possessed. They had interests in the Balkans, Anatolia, Iran, Iraq and along the North African coast. The significance of Jerusalem could only dwindle in this vast perspective. Above all, the Ottoman capital was in Istanbul, not Cairo, and in an age of slow, laborious communications this effectively rendered Jerusalem out of sight, out of mind. Moreover, the principal theatres of war in Ottoman times were the Balkans, Iran, the Mediterranean—Palestine fomented a minor rebellion on occasion, but nothing to justify the intervention of the imperial army in force. After a brief spate of Ottoman interest in the city in the generation after the conquest in 1517—a period which saw most of the significant Ottoman contributions to the city's architectural heritage—Jerusalem sank to the status of a minor provincial town. It lost touch with the great world. An economy long boosted by the intense building activity of the Mamluk period gradually stagnated. The city turned inwards, resting on its past glories while its current affairs gradually became the preserve of a few leading local Arab families who dominated the religious establishment and the administration of the *waqfs* of its many pious foundations.

Even in the Levant itself, Jerusalem under the Ottomans was significantly downgraded *vis-à-vis* its role a century earlier. Under the Mamluks, Damascus and Aleppo were indeed more important politically, yet Jerusalem rivalled them in its architectural heritage because of the special religious significance which it held to that dynasty. Under the Ottomans, Damascus and Aleppo, in accordance with their much larger populations and their greater political and economic importance, were both graced with many major buildings. This was not true of Jerusalem. And thus a paradox emerges: the Ottomans disposed of much larger cash revenues than did the Mamluks, and—as already noted—ruled Jerusalem for considerably longer, and yet they built far less; and what they did build was on a much smaller scale. This can only mean that they gave Jerusalem a lower priority than did the Mamluks. Yet the city was by no means neglected; and it is one of the ironies of its history that under the early Ottomans its population tripled, a process perhaps due in part to Sultan Sulaiman's repair in 1532 of the aqueduct originally built by the Amir Tankiz, who was Viceroy of Syria between 1312 and 1340. The restoration of the aqueduct was completed in 1541-2; it conducted water from the Pools of Solomon (Birkat Sulaiman, three pools south of Bethlehem), to certain *hammams* in the city, to nine public fountains in Jerusalem, and to others on the Haram. The central religious importance of water in the ablutions preceding prayer should be borne in mind here. Indeed, a passage of Evliya Çelebi, the indefatigable 17th-century Ottoman traveller, suggests that the provision of water to the Haram was the prime motive of the massive investment in hydraulic works, and in fact all the channels terminated in the Haram. Sulaiman's reconstruction and enlargement of the bazaar area

revitalised the urban economy, and did much to alleviate the city's chronic water shortage, with its accompanying threat of disease. But it also had wider horizons—thus the new spice bazaar was part of the Ottoman response to the challenge which Portuguese activities in the Indian Ocean presented to the lucrative spice trade, traditionally a Mamluk monopoly. Above all, Sulaiman's rebuilding of the walls resulted in a complete circuit of fortifications and thereby set Jerusalem apart from most other Palestinian towns, which would have created a welcome sense of security and thus an added incentive to settle there.

Unlike today, when much of the Mamluk heritage has vanished altogether and most of what remains is dilapidated or diminished by later constructions, in 1517 and the following few decades it must have been largely intact, for the most part of recent origin and of a splendour that was very plainly hard to beat. These buildings, and sometimes the structures surrounding them too, were still well protected by functioning *waqfs* which prevented unauthorised re-use or adaptation. All this may well have made the Ottomans disinclined to enter into retrospective competition with the Mamluk achievement; but it may also have suggested to them that the city simply did not need an architectural transformation. The afterglow of Mamluk patronage must have lingered for generations. Its implicit challenge helps to explain why the best Ottoman architecture in Jerusalem is concentrated into the 16th century—though it is only fair to note that in the Ottoman capital, Istanbul, this was also the period, broadly coinciding with the reign of Sulaiman the Magnificent, the longest in Ottoman history, which saw the apogee of Ottoman architecture. The fact that Jerusalem was still a relatively new Ottoman possession may also have played its part as an incentive for architectural activity.

A consistent feature of Ottoman architecture in Jerusalem, and one which is not nearly as marked in the Mamluk period, is the steady emphasis on restoration work. Thus, for example, the Ottoman contribution to the upkeep of the fabric of the Aqsa Mosque and the Dome of the Rock deserves a chapter to itself. It seems to have been a consistent Ottoman practice to keep the architectural heritage of the Mamluks in good repair. The *sijills*—registers or archives of the Muslim religious court in Jerusalem, which run to some 650 volumes containing about 100,000 folios—are an excellent source for the details of this activity and they document how very widespread it was. They show, for example, that a proportion of *waqf* income was regularly set aside to pay for repairs, whether these comprised the restoration of a wall or new building (*'amara*) or merely the renewal of mortar or the repair of doors (*tarmim*). Responsibility for the oversight of such work, and for granting permission that it be done, lay with the officials under the jurisdiction of the *qadi*. He presided over the committee of enquiry (which typically included master builders in its membership) that inspected a property before repairs were sanctioned. The wider picture that emerges from these details is of a steadfast long-term commitment by the local Ottoman authorities to maintaining the fabric of the city's buildings in optimum condition.

On the whole the Mamluk *amir*s had concentrated their building activity on the immediate surroundings of the Haram, and this area gradually filled up with public monuments in the course of the Mamluk centuries. Thus by 1517 there was virtually no room left for further significant construction in this part of the city—quite apart from the fact that it effectively bore the stamp of Mamluk ownership. There was only one place left for the new dynasty—the interior of the Haram—and, for all the difficulties that this site presented, the Ottomans were so to speak in honour bound to use it. But the ineluctable need to respect the Dome of the Rock and the Aqsa Mosque and not to intrude on their physical space in any way seriously inhibited prospective Ottoman patrons. One cannot help being struck by how low the Ottoman buildings on the Haram are in comparison with the Mamluk façades which border it; they are dwarfed in comparison. Yet as the new masters of Jerusalem they had to assert their power in some tangible, visible, architectural way. That political imperative—so often a factor in glamorous public architecture—excluded foundations in the outskirts of the city, where they would have been effectively out of sight, and pointed, so far as religious architecture was concerned, to the hitherto unexploited Haram. In the field of secular architecture, on the other hand, there was one obvious task to be undertaken, and it was one which the Mamluks had sedulously ignored: the rebuilding of the walls.

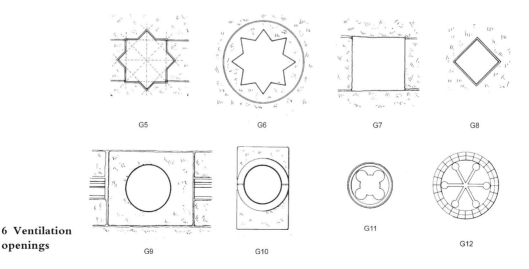

6 Ventilation openings

G5   G6   G7   G8

G9   G10   G11   G12

18

3   THE CITY WALLS

3.1 Introduction

Beyond question, the most striking testimony of Ottoman architectural patronage in Jerusalem is the circuit of walls repaired and in part erected by Sulaiman the Magnificent between 1537 and 1541, as its thirteen inscriptions record (colour pl. XVI). That epigraphic evidence is central to an assessment of Sulaiman's contribution to the walls, for the exact state of these walls at the time of the Ottoman conquest is still a matter of lively controversy, with opinions divided on the degree to which their fabric was ruined, and thus on whether Sulaiman's work tended more towards repair or towards new construction. Even though for the most part they rest on earlier foundations, and indeed (as Meinecke notes) in their rectangular towers and their gates with dog-leg entrance passages directly recall Ayyubid and Mamluk military technology (the city walls of Damascus, Aleppo and even Cairo furnish ample parallels), five years is still an astoundingly short time for a project on this scale. That fact alone speaks volumes for the efficiency of the Ottoman administration. It is of course possible that work on the walls began before the earliest of the inscriptions and ended after the latest of them; but it was customary for inscriptions to mark the completion of an architectural task and the cumulative evidence of so many dated inscriptions is not lightly to be gainsaid. The supervisor and financial administrator of the entire enterprise was Muhammad Çelebi al-Naqqash, whose title ('the designer' or 'the painter') suggests that his professional competence extended far beyond architecture. Indeed, his responsibilities included the collection of the poll-tax *(jizya)* levied on non-Muslims, a particularly important duty in Jerusalem of all cities.

3.2 The report of Evliya Çelebi

Evliya Çelebi attributes this massive enterprise to a dream of Sultan Sulaiman in which the Prophet appeared to him and told him to use the booty from his successful campaigns to embellish Mecca and Madina and to fortify the Citadel of Jerusalem, embellish the Haram and rebuild the city itself. The trustworthiness of this colourful account is marred by several egregious errors, but that is scarcely to the purpose, for this picturesque story is of special interest because it serves to contextualise the reconstruction of the city walls. Three key elements may be distinguished here: the presentation of the Sultan as the one who shouldered the cost of the project; the fact that building activity in Mecca and Madina is mentioned as part and parcel of the same sacred commission; and that the walls are not specifically mentioned at all. It is worth investigating these aspects in turn in a little more detail.

How, then, were these enterprises financed? What actually happened was that Palestine itself, including to a modest extent the population of Jerusalem, was laid under contribution by means of taxes for the cost of these public works. These were supplemented by contribution from Istanbul and Damascus. It is surely no accident that the years 1525-6 and 1538 saw the land registration of Syria and Palestine, a process which firmly established the central

7 The Dome of the Rock from the city wall towards the Maghribi Gate (Dung Gate) in 1858
(Francis Frith, Library of Congress)

8 Walls of the city from the Birkat Mamilla and cemetery in 1857. A mausoleum from the Mamluk period is
visible to the left of the pool (M J Diness, Scottish National Portrait Gallery, Edinburgh).

overriding authority of the sultan and, as a direct consequence of this, facilitated the collection of revenue. Moreover, between 932/1525-6 and 961/1553-4 the population of the city tripled, and with it the taxation base. If the transformation of the city by Sulaiman cannot be seen as the principal engine of this demographic turnaround, it surely played a major part in the process, making Jerusalem an attractive, prestigious and much safer place in which to live. New housing, not just the bringing back into use of dilapidated property, was a priority, and this goes far to explain the buoyancy of the building trade in the second quarter of the 16th century in Jerusalem. Water supply, physical security, commercial services, pilgrimage facilities—all coalesced at one time and place, with transforming effect. They have to be seen together, for they represent much more than the sum of their parts.

The links with Mecca and Madina, which have already been mentioned in Chapter 2, are a complex issue. Sulaiman was described by the *mufti* of Istanbul, Ebu Su'ud Efendi, as 'Protector of the holy ground of the Two Sanctuaries' and he bore, like successive Ottoman sultans, the title 'Servant of the Two Sanctuaries' *(khadim al-haramain)*. In a letter to the Habsburg Emperor Ferdinand in 1554 Sulaiman described himself as ruler of Mecca, Madina and Jerusalem, thereby bracketing all three cities together in a special category of their own. He thus went somewhat further than the traditional title allowed, and his extensive patronage in all three cities—all far away from his capital—fleshed out that claim in an unmistakably public and practical manner. A document of 1565 takes up this theme anew with its reference to his lordship of 'Mecca the venerated, Madina the illuminated and Jerusalem the noble'. This helps to put his building activity in Jerusalem—as distinct from his foundations in Baghdad, Damascus, Aleppo, Edirne, Konya and elsewhere—into a specifically and pan-Islamic pious context. In Madina—whose water supply, like that of Mecca, was the responsibility of a

specially appointed official, a salaried Inspector of Waterworks—he repaired the Mosque of the Prophet, coating the dome over the tomb of the Prophet with lead, replacing the existing finial with a larger gilded one (946/1539), paving the floor of the mosque with coloured marble and (in 948/1541) rebuilding the wooden western *mihrab* (of 860/1455-6) there, al-Mihrab al-Sulaimaniyya, by encasing it in marble and making it match the eastern *mihrab*. He also rebuilt the Treasury of the Prophet in 974/1566. His works at Mecca were rather more extensive. He constructed an aqueduct, for as at Jerusalem, but to an even greater extent, the need to provide this basic necessity for pilgrims was paramount. He also endowed four *madrasa*s there; repaired two minarets at the Haram and added a seventh, the tallest of all; and (as at Madina) endowed a soup kitchen *('imaret)* in memory of his wife Khurram/Hürrem—the very same type of building which she herself endowed in Jerusalem and which was also incorporated in the complex built in her name in Istanbul in 945/1538-9. In the cases of Mecca, Madina and Jerusalem—unlike the parallel contemporary royal foundations of this kind in Cairo and Damascus—it may be assumed that the founder had the welfare of pilgrims in mind. Moreover, Sulaiman also started the major enterprise of rebuilding the arcades which surrounded the courtyard in which the Ka'ba was set; indeed, these repairs, which continued after his death, gave the Meccan Haram the aspect which it wore until the early 20th century. The columns bound with iron bands and bearing *muqarnas* capitals probably date from his building campaigns; they have numerous parallels in Ottoman Jerusalem. In 956/1549 he also donated a marble *minbar* almost as high as the Ka'ba, and with a gilded roof. South of the Haram he erected a further *madrasa* in 972/1565.

These initiatives in the three Holy Cities of Islam continued a policy begun in Ottoman times by Selim I, a policy which had already been pursued by such Mamluk rulers as Baibars (who had carried out repair work on the Prophet's

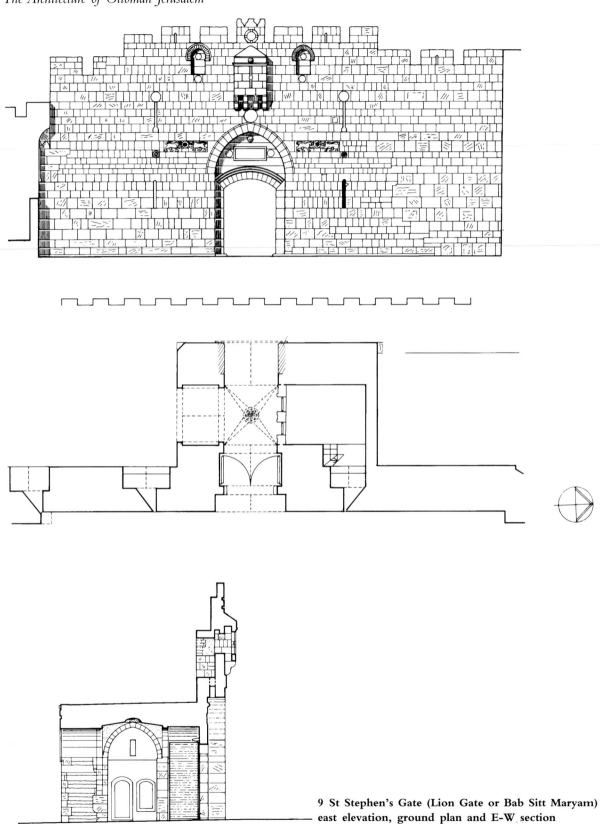

9 St Stephen's Gate (Lion Gate or Bab Sitt Maryam) east elevation, ground plan and E-W section

10 The Citadel of Jerusalem—aerial perespective

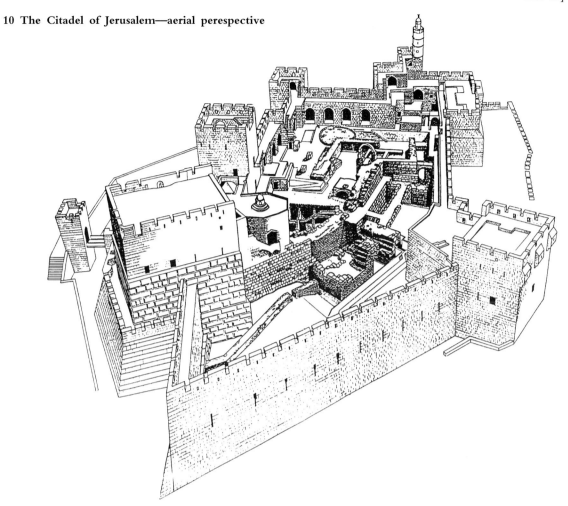

11 The citadel of Jerusalem, barbican looking north

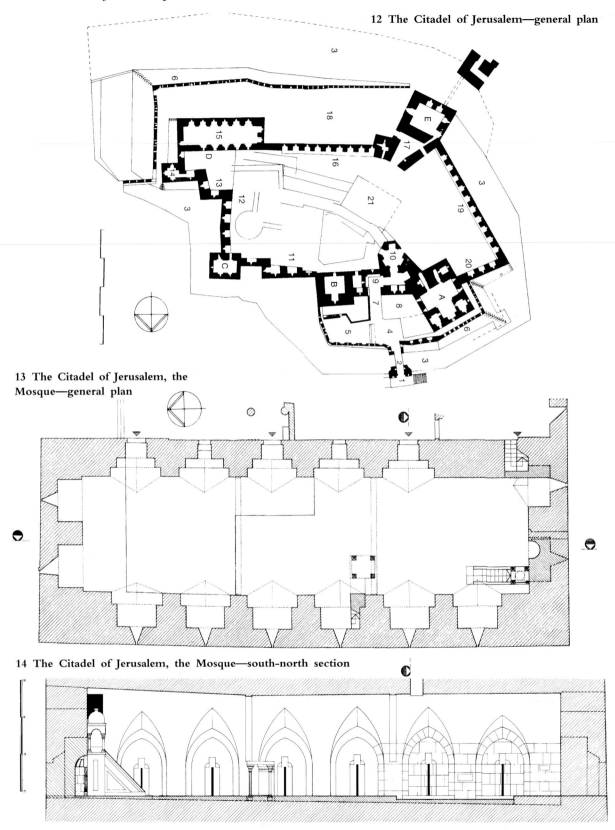

12 The Citadel of Jerusalem—general plan

13 The Citadel of Jerusalem, the Mosque—general plan

14 The Citadel of Jerusalem, the Mosque—south-north section

Mosque at Madina and at the Dome of the Rock) and Qa'it Bay (who had patronised major buildings, repairs or significant additions in all three Holy Cities). But they also had a deeper topical dimension in that they responded in kind to the aggressive promotion of Shi'ism by the major enemy of the Ottomans in the Islamic world—the Safavid Shah Isma'il I. Some of the most dangerous internal rebellions which Sulaiman had to quell, such as the Qizilbash insurrections of 1526 and 1527, were also of Shi'ite character. The four *madrasa*s at Mecca (dedicated, like their counterparts in the Sulaimaniyya complex at Istanbul, to all four *madhhab*s) fitted into this pattern, serving as they did to propagate Sunni orthodoxy and the legitimacy of Ottoman rule by the agency of state-appointed *'ulama'*.

Next, the story does not directly mention the walls. It is 'the fortification of the citadel of Jerusalem' that is specifically mentioned, as is the more general command to 'rebuild Jerusalem'. The Citadel and the Tower of David had been demolished in 637/1239 to prevent their falling into Frankish hands, and then rebuilt by the Mamluk Sultan al-Nasir Muhammad, as documented by two inscriptions dated 710/1310, some two decades after the final defeat of the Crusaders. Evliya Çelebi, writing well over a century after the event, was of course well placed to know that the Citadel had indeed been comprehensively rebuilt at the order of Sultan Sulaiman. This was his first major act of architectural patronage in the city; the work was begun in 938/1531, and the *sijills* show that three master builders supervised the inspection of its walls. An epigraphic roundel of unmistakably Mamluk type—though it lacks the slender grace of the typical royal Mamluk roundel—and in the name of Sultan Sulaiman is located above the *mihrab* in the Summer Mosque of the Citadel. It suggests by purely visual means the seamless transition from Mamluk to Ottoman power, a political message of no mean substance. Since the Citadel, while adjoining the walls, is separately defensible, it was the obvious

15 The Citadel, medallion on stone bridge

place to begin in the overall scheme of making Jerusalem more secure, whether—as will shortly be discussed—from European threats or those from the local Beduin. As the base for the local Ottoman commander, it was also a suitable and permanent reminder to the people of Jerusalem that Ottoman rule had decisively replaced that of the Mamluks, whose garrison had occupied the citadel until 1516. As for the reference to the rebuilding of Jerusalem, this is too vague to bear detailed interpretation. But the *sijills*, which have been combed for evidence of Ottoman building activity in Jerusalem in the first half of the 16th century, do not yield evidence for a large-scale housing programme within the city sponsored by the state rather than by local people. So how can the word 'rebuild' be construed? The wider picture reveals that the reconstruction of the walls was not only a vital preliminary to further work in the city, in that it guaranteed the permanence of such work, but also effectively an apt symbol of the revival of the city under Ottoman rule. It may not be too bold a speculation, therefore, to understand the work on the walls as subsumed in the more general notion of rebuilding Jerusalem.

The tale told by Evliya Çelebi is interesting on two further counts. It places Jerusalem implicitly on a par with Madina, in that Sulaiman is said to have despatched equal sums—a thousand purses of his own money—to each. Perhaps the fact that he built a wall around these two cities is a

16 False joints cut in the masonry of the city wall south of Bab al-Asbat (St Stephen's Gate)

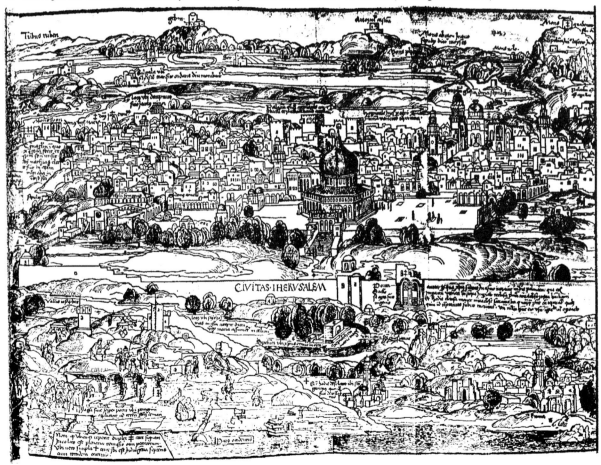

17 Edward Reuwich of Utrecht's view of Jerusalem, from Bernard of Breydenbach, *Pergrinationes in Terram Sanctam* (1486)

relevant factor here. Moreover, while in the dream the Prophet tells Sulaiman to embellish Mecca as well, there is no mention here of his sending a specific sum for that purpose. Yet his work at Mecca was more extensive than at Madina.

Evliya Çelebi, writing a good century after the events he purports to recount, is of necessity not a reliable witness, quite apart from his decision to cast a legendary afterglow over the events themselves by using the device of a dream not mentioned in strictly contemporary accounts. But what is 'remembered' by later generations is of course no less important than what 'happened', for it reflects the perennially protean nature of Jerusalem as a symbol to Muslims no less than to Christians and Jews.

3.3 The historical and contemporary context of the rebuilding programme

It is now time to look more closely at the Ottoman rebuilding of the city's walls. Several introductory remarks may be in order. First, this was a rare accolade for the Holy City, since its walls had been in an increasingly ruinous condition ever since their deliberate breach by the Ayyubid princes al-Mu'azzam 'Isa and al-Malik al-Kamil in 1219 and 1227 to prevent their use by the Christian enemy. The Franciscan father Noë Bianco reported on his visit to Jerusalem in 1527 that the walls were almost in ruins; clearly, for all their devotion to the city, the Mamluks had stopped short at rebuilding the entire circuit of its walls. Second, fully walled cities—as distinct from fortified citadels dominating unwalled cities, as was the case at Aleppo and Damascus—were a rarity in the Near East. One reason for this was, no doubt, that fluctuations in the density of settlement within a city tended either to result in expansion beyond the city walls, thus making those walls an encumbrance, or to render parts of the walls redundant and dangerously

18 St Stephen's Gate (Bab Sitt Maryam) in 1870 (photograph © Elia Photographic Services)

19 The interior of the Damascus Gate (Bab al-'Amud) in 1935 (photograph © Elia Photographic Services)

exposed, since the population had diminished and had left tracts of the city sparsely occupied or even deserted. Third, these walls largely followed the line of earlier walls erected when the city was more densely populated, and thus the Ottoman walls defined the area of Jerusalem generously, leaving plenty of room for renewed population growth and thus expressing faith in the future of the city. And for the first time in centuries they gave Jerusalem a physical unity—the necessary prelude to a more intangible sense of community and morale. Fourth, there is a more than local context here, for at almost the same time the selfsame Sultan Sulaiman was constructing a major wall around Madina, the second holiest city in Islam; and of course, his capital, the former Constantinople, was itself surrounded by late Roman and Byzantine walls which were one of the wonders of the medieval world. That fact, and the perennial association of those walls with great empires of

27

20 The Damascus Gate, the only northern entrance to the Old City when photographed by
Bonfils in the mid-1860s (Bonfils, Collection of Fouad Debbas, Paris)

21 Jaffa Gate *c.* 1860 with its
unpaved approach and unbreached
wall to the left (Peter Bergheim,
Library of Congress)

antiquity, might well have motivated Sulaiman to emulate that achievement elsewhere, and to present himself as a latter-day Caesar. Lastly, it would be mistaken to attribute this costly project entirely to the pious motives of the sultan. Other factors, both local and international, were at work.

The local factors were not confined to the city. Jerusalem, in common with Hebron and other Palestinian towns, had long suffered from the raids which marauding Beduin tribes regularly conducted against travellers on the open road and even against the inhabitants of the outskirts of the larger towns. Thus a chronic insecurity afflicted the surrounding countryside for much of the Ottoman period, even though the *sijill*s record the appointments of officials as late as 1256/1840 charged with the protection of travellers and the repair of access roads to the city. Hence there is a darker side to the building of these walls. Put briefly, the building of the walls absolved the Ottoman authorities of the need to police the environs of Jerusalem effectively, and indeed could be interpreted as an acknowledgment that the writ of the government did not run in these areas. This was not a new situation; early in the 16th century, at the end of the Mamluk period, no one could perform the *hajj* from Jerusalem for an entire decade because the Beduin had rendered the roads so unsafe. Beduin lawlessness in fact persisted for centuries and the protection of travellers, for example on the main Ramla-Jerusalem road, necessitated the provision of a heavy guard or the payment of protection money. As late as the early 18th century the then governor of Jerusalem, Mustafa Agha, negotiated an agreement with the inhabitants of a trio of villages to the north of Jerusalem that they would not molest travellers bound for the city. This context of chronic insecurity also helps to explain the provision of strategically sited gates which allowed the authorities to control access to the city.

The story does not end here: there is an international dimension too. After the defining and traumatic experience of the Crusades, it is no wonder that in Muslim eyes the Christian pilgrims who continued to visit Jerusalem should represent the shadow of a possible threat against the city, all the more so as the Europeans had never abjured the resumption of hostilities. In the 1530s, rumours were circulating of a new crusade under the leadership of the Holy Roman Emperor Charles V, stung by the recent Ottoman campaigns in Austria. In the aftermath of the fall of Rhodes, the last Christian outpost in the Levant, in 1520, such rumours could not be ignored, and indeed Charles did mount an expedition against Algiers in 1538. Its failure may explain why work on the walls of Jerusalem was abruptly terminated, leaving the interiors of about half the towers unfinished. Nevertheless, the scale and nature of Ottoman work on the towers can be gauged by the Stork, Gaza and Sulphur Towers, and by Goliath's Castle.

3.4 Features of construction

Some of this work was executed on earlier foundations; on occasion this earlier masonry had to be levelled to facilitate new construction. The unfinished state of the work—for while the circuit of the walls is complete, neither the height nor the treatment of the ramparts themselves is consistent—is perhaps not all that serious a deficiency, since the role of these walls was at least as much symbolic as military. In that respect they follow a long Islamic tradition, recorded from as early as Umayyad times, of walls whose strength is more apparent than real. They represented a *prise de possession* and a deterrent to any Christian designs on the city. It is certain that they would not long have resisted a determined attack by an enemy force equipped with up-to-date artillery: at some points, admittedly, the walls are almost three metres thick at the base, with a glacis in some places, but they are on the whole less than 1.5 metres thick at the level of loopholes and less than half that thickness at the height of the ramparts—a level at which the lateral thrust exerted against the lower parts of the wall by the earth itself and by substructures is no longer a factor. This reduction is sometimes managed by a succession of retreating jogs. Thus the upper sections of the wall, festooned as they are with bosses, parapets and merlons, are largely for show—hence for example the sudden outcrop of decorative forms in the battlements of the Damascus Gate—though they would assuredly have foiled any attacks by raiding Beduin. They would have sufficed for small-arms fire, but not for artillery. To that extent the many gunports are deceptive. Their irregular placing is also somewhat inconsistent with a military function. Numerous staircases give access to the upper part of the walls. The variations in height—from 5 to 15 metres approximately(that is 17 to 50 feet)—tell the same story of protection against casual raids rather than a professional army with state-of-the-art cannons.

The pace of work was notably uneven. This was partly because, as noted above, there was no attempt to rebuild the walls from scratch; earlier sections of finished wall, from pre-Herodian times onwards, were incorporated without change wherever possible. No doubt debris from demolished or ruinous buildings in the immediate vicinity of the wall was used wherever possible. These factors explain the extremely varied stonework, which ranges from the cyclopean blocks of the ancient foundations to the small, neat and relatively uniform squares which characterise Ottoman work. The earlier wall-lines were used wherever this was practicable, as were the existing ditches—though when the French ambassador to Istanbul, Le Chevalier d'Aramon, visited Jerusalem in 1549 he noted the absence of a moat (an unreasonable expectation in view of the local climate and topography). The uneven preservation of the earlier walls, together with the variable terrain, are among the factors which explain why the work did not proceed at a steady rate. Indeed, the construction of a mere 600 metres of the wall from the area of David's Gate (Zion Gate) to the south end of the Citadel took 22 months—about half the entire time required for the project as a whole to be carried to completion. The Ottoman masons paid their ancient predecessors the compliment of imitation, displaying at the same time a notable awareness of visual consistency, for they frequently took the trouble to incise false horizontal and vertical joints on earlier blocks of stone in an attempt fictively to reduce their dimensions to something close to the Ottoman norm. Much earlier masonry was also incorporated into the filling of the wall, with the better-preserved stones (some of them bearing pre-Ottoman inscriptions) being re-used for the facing. The researches of Burgoyne show that the typical Ottoman masonry technique favoured a pocked surface with rough marginal drafting and a standard size of block—clear evidence of strong centralised control of the quarrying and finishing processes. The work-force was divided into unskilled labourers, those who cut the stone (*nahhat*), those who dressed it (*hajjar*) and finally the builders themselves (*banna'*). The most numerous of these were certainly the labourers, for a comment by the Madinese scholar al-Khiyari, who visited the city in 1669, mentions the trench in front of the city walls, and the digging of this feature would have been a major part of the entire building campaign.

3.5 The scope of the project

Some basic facts will clarify the size and ambition of the whole enterprise. If all the angles, re-entrants, towers and gates are included in the calculation, they extend a total of 4.325 km (2.7 miles). For some reason Mount Zion was excluded, despite its strategic importance, and the Citadel, itself of Mamluk origin, which, as already mentioned, Sulaiman had fortified and garrisoned as early as 1531, had its own system of defences, though in places these blend with the outer city walls. Like many a medieval monarch before him, then, Sulaiman's first concern was to establish a strong military presence in the city. The military aspect of the walls, at least so far as their overall visual impact is concerned, is driven home by no less than 34 towers, which vary in their height, design and angle of fire. These are supplemented by 344 loopholes or embrasures intended for gunfire, by numerous angles to give enfilading fire (Evliya Çelebi noted 'seventy-three bends which command other walls'), and by 17 machicolations, some of them clearly intended in a decorative spirit to judge by the *muqarnas* decoration or corbels with roll mouldings at their base. Indeed, their overall shape itself has an aesthetic dimension, for they were apparently conceived as a series of variations on a theme: some straddle V-shaped projections in the wall, others are plain rectangular boxes topped by a flat or pitched roof, while still others take the form of half-cylinders adorned with crenellations. Similarly, the crenellations like tiny domed aedicules which crown the merlons at key spots like the Damascus Gate function as ornament; they have no possible military purpose. There are seven open gates, all but one of them inscribed with the date of their construction. In some cases earlier Mamluk elements are incorporated in secondary use, perhaps for talismanic purposes as in the lions—the heraldic symbol of Sultan Baibars, the scourge of the Crusaders—which flank St Stephen's Gate, otherwise known as the Lion Gate. Four older gates—the Golden, Single, Double and Triple Gates—lend still further monumentality to the ensemble, though the latter three gates, being located under the south wall of the Aqsa Mosque, are not strictly part of the city walls. The Golden Gate itself was largely rebuilt under the Ottomans. Access to the two main thoroughfares which bisect Jerusalem is through the four major gates: Jaffa, Lion, Damascus and Zion (or Sion), but Herod's Gate and the Dung Gate, to the north and south respectively, handled the overflow of traffic and offered supplementary entrances to other parts of the city. Thus the Ottoman walls were carefully planned to be integrated with the gates and thus to facilitate communications, both within the city itself and between the city and its hinterland.

Building on this scale taxed local resources in both cash and craftsmen well beyond their natural limits. Thus over the five-year campaign (1536-40) the whole of Palestine and even some of Syria was laid under contribution to supplement the expenditure incurred from central government funds. The *sijills* of the Shari'a Court for the year 945/1538 give details of this, and other *sijills* give details of the the types of stone and mortar used on the walls, and their sources. Not surprisingly, Jerusalem itself was too small to provide the entirety of the work force, and craftsmen were imported from as far afield as Cairo and Aleppo. Sijill 12 mentions that Muhammad Çelebi al-Naqqash, the superintendent in charge of building the walls, borrowed 10,000 *'uthmani*s from the Jew Ibrahim Castro (to whom he had earlier sold saffron, evidence that his activities were not entirely architectural) on the occasion of a visit to Cairo 'to meet the architects in connection with the walls'. This sum was roughly equivalent to 250 gold *sultani*s. That same superintendent, arraigned for negligence in the construction of the walls at the end of the whole project by reason of the collapse of equipment and materials in the western section of the wall, was generously exonerated in court by Darwish, one of the master builders from Aleppo who had worked on the wall. The actual words of Darwish are recorded: 'I was with him for four years and I never saw anything objectionable about him, so how at the end of the work can I write a complaint against him?' Sijill 12 indicates that detailed records of the income and expenditure associated with the entire project of the walls were kept.

For reasons of security, work began on the north side, which was the most vulnerable, and ended on the west side. The urgency with which the project was driven forward helps to explain not only the short cuts outlined above but also the frequent use of *spolia*. That same desire to save time and expense explains why some of the roundels and circular medallions which ornament the walls at irregular intervals (for instance in the area of the Damascus Gate) turn out on close inspection to be the re-carved ends of cylindrical columns inserted into the walls as strengthening devices. Most of the carved roundels, however, were cut from square blocks specifically for use on the walls. Numerous inscribed plaques document the progress of construction; the bare facts and dates are interspersed with verses of thanksgiving. The walls of course have their later history, notably the alterations to the New and Dung Gates, to the glacis and to the moat of the Citadel in the course of the 18th and 19th centuries; but their form today is sufficiently close to the way that Sulaiman's engineers left them. That form effectively crystallised the image of the city in the minds of later generations, and also kept the municipal development of the city within the perimeter of those walls until the population explosion of the later 19th century. The role of the walls in fostering a sense of community in its citizens despite their conflicting confessional loyalties is not the least of the achievements of Sulaiman the Magnificent.

I *Haram al-Sharif, with Dome of the Rock and the Aqsa Mosque,* Hajj Vekaletnamesi, *951/1544-45, Topkapi Sarayi Library.*

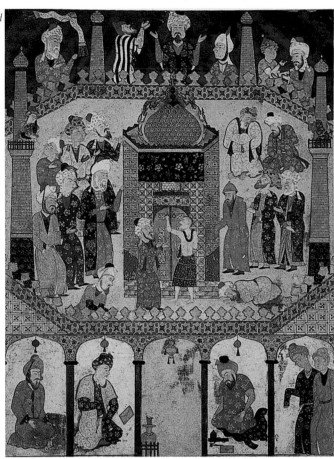

II *Dervishes and the Dome of the Rock, Falnama, attributed to Aqa Mirak. Tabriz 1550, Pozzi Collection, Musée d'Art ed d'Histoire, Geneva, no. 1971-107/34.*

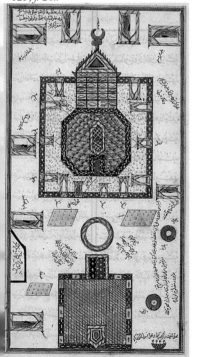

III *Haram al-Sharif, with Dome of the Rock and the Aqsa Mosque,* Nur al-Vahhaj li tahsil al-ilaj, *1253/1857, Ms. Vat. Turco 125, f. 26r.*

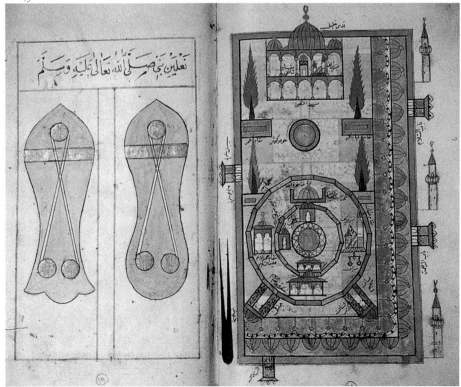

IV *Sandals of the Prophet and the Haram al-Sharif, Jerusalem, National and University Library, Yah. ms. Ar. 117, f. 41r.*

V *Examples of original 16th-century glazed bricks used to screen the windows of the Dome of the Rock, removed in 1966 (Photo John Carswell)*

VI *Three underglaze tile panels, used in subsequent repairs to the Dome of the Rock; two are dated, AH 1233 and AH 1234. Probably Syrian manufacture (Photo John Carswell).*

VIII *(Top) Four cuerda seca 16th-century tiles, removed in 1966. (Bottom) A tile showing the transition from cuerda seca to true underglaze decoration (Photo John Carswell).*

VII *Decorated tiles from Sulaiman's 16th-century restoration, removed in 1966 (Photo John Carswell)*

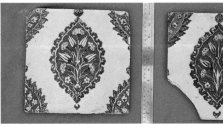

IX *Detail of a cuerda seca tile from the Dome of the Rock, c. 1560 (Photo John Carswell)*

X *Two rare imported Iznik tiles used in the redecoration of the Dome of the Rock, c. 1560. Removed in 1966 (Photo John Carswell)*

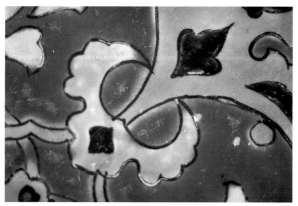

XI *Detail of a cuerda seca tile from the Dome of the Rock, c. 1560 (Photo John Carswell)*

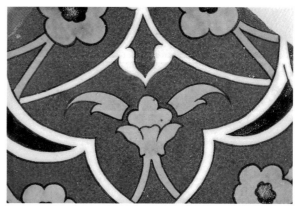

XII *Tile from the Dome of the Rock, c. 1560 (detail) (Photo John Carswell)*

XIII *Detail of ceiling, decoration with baroqwr quatrelobe outline and bamboo octagon, from Coptic Patriarchate, Old City (Photo Sharif al-Sharif).*

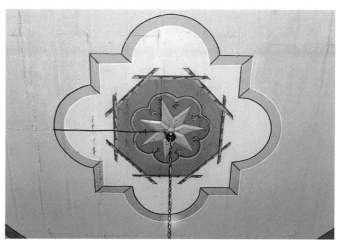

XIV *Hujrat Islam Beg, west elevation*

XV *The Dome of the Rock during the latter part of the restoration work of the late 1960s. In the foreground, Qubbat al-Arwah (Photo Alistair Duncan).*

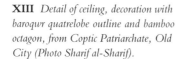

XVI *This study of the (essentially) Ottoman Holy City was taken before the aesthetic and integrated balance of the skyline was marred by high-rise buildings in the second half of the 20th century (Photo Alistair Duncan).*

XVII *Hujrat Islam Beg, south elevation*

XVIII *Dar al-Bairam Jawish, looking north, built as a* qantara *above Tariq al-Wad.*

XIX *North-west Khalwa of Ahmad Pasha, view of south and east façades with further* khalwas *in the background.*

XX *North-west Khalwa of Ahmad Pasha, internal doorway*

XXI *North-west Khalwa of Ahmad Pasha, east façade*

XXII *Pavilion or iwan of Sultan Mahmud II (Photo Michael Burgoyne)*

XXIII *Qubbat Yusuf (Photo Michael Burgoyne)*

XXIV *Qubbat al-Nabi with Dome of the Rock in the background (Photo Michael Burgoyne)*

XXV *Mihrab ʿAli Pasha, inscription*

XXVI *Mastaba and Sabil Mustafa Agha. The* mastaba *is also known as Mastabat al-Basiri and the* sabil *as Sabil al-Shaikh Budair (Photo Michael Burgoyne).*

XXVIII *Sabil Mustafa Agha (al-Shaikh Budair) (Photo Michael Burgoyne)*

XXVII *Sabil Mustafa Agha (al-Shaikh Budair), detail of SW column*

XXIX *North-west Khalwa of Ahmad Pasha*

XXX *North-west Khalwa of Ahmad Pasha*

XXXI *Sabil Tariq Bab al-Nazir (Photo Michael Burgoyne)*

XXXII *Sabil Bab al-Silsila (Photo Michael Burgoyne)*

4 THE ROLE OF JERUSALEM IN THE OTTOMAN LEVANTINE CONTEXT

4.1 Jerusalem in the general context of Near Eastern cities

While there is no question that in matters of religious significance Jerusalem was unchallenged by any other city in the Levant, and was outranked only by Mecca and Madina in the Islamic world at large, its political and economic role was quite another matter. Egypt, in Ottoman as in medieval times, was the major force in the south-east Mediterranean, and was thus in many ways a law to itself. Comparisons with the major cities of the Levant in Ottoman times, namely Aleppo and Damascus, are therefore more to the point. Jerusalem shared with these cities the formula traditionally followed in Arab cities, whereby public buildings were concentrated in the city centre criss-crossed by major arteries, with the private residential zone further out and linked by smaller, irregular streets, alleys and *culs-de-sac*. But the main fact to bear in mind is that, by the standards of the major Levantine cities, Jerusalem for most of the Ottoman period was tiny, both in its physical scale *intra muros* and in terms of its population. In about 1525 Damascus, even after the destruction inflicted on it by Timur a little over a century earlier, had, according to the Ottoman registers, a population of approximately 57,000. In that same year, those registers show that Jerusalem had a population of some 4,000 inhabitants; this tripled during the reign of Sulaiman the Magnificent, but incompetent government and a resultant decline in revenues—for the city was essentially a tax farm administered by Ottoman officials in Egypt, Sidon or Damascus for their own benefit—steadily impoverished most of the inhabitants. This very small population

suggests that, while there might well have been pockets of dense habitation in the area around the Haram, Ottoman Jerusalem as a whole cannot have been heavily built up. Supporting evidence for this assertion comes from the *waqf* of the Qadiriyya Zawiya, which mentions a big square *haud* for plantation and 'a fair *hakura* (orchard) situated to the east of the *zawiya*, approached from the *zawiya* and planted with figs, almonds and grapevines'. By 1806 the number of inhabitants was estimated at 8,000, at a time when Aleppo had a population perhaps approaching 100,000; this represents a significant decline from earlier Ottoman times, for Raymond, analysing in depth the data provided by D'Arvieux for 1683, and noting the rapid growth of the town's suburbs during the 16th and 17th centuries, estimates that the population of Aleppo at that time was slightly under 115,000.

It is well to ponder these figures, and the economy which they reflect, when one tries to find an adequate context for Ottoman Jerusalem and its architecture. To put it brutally, the city was poor, and such money as it generated came mainly from non-Muslims. In the 16th century the two major sources of government revenue in the city were the toll levied on visitors to the Holy Sepulchre and the poll-tax imposed on Christians and Jews. The two-stage conversion of a local Christian church into the mosque of al-Nabi Da'ud, a process completed in 930/1524, illustrates another aspect of this anti-Christian policy.

The commercial activity of the local Arab population could not begin to compete with that of Damascus or Aleppo, and therefore could not support the kind of building programmes undertaken in those cities. It is therefore no wonder

22 Masjid al-Nabi Da'ud, general view with bell-tower of Dormition church in the background

23 Masjid al-Nabi Da'ud, window. 24 Masjid al-Nabi Da'ud, window. 25 Masjid al-Nabi Da'ud, *mihrab.*

that the patrons for the buildings of Ottoman Jerusalem belonged largely to the Turkish governing class. Moreover, the relative obscurity of Jerusalem in this period and the short tenure of office which these officials could expect in turn meant that they did not on the whole wield significant power or wealth; they were not rich grandees by the standards of Damascus or Aleppo, let alone Istanbul. All this helps to explain why the buildings of Ottoman Jerusalem are so modest in scale and decoration. A wider context for these buildings can be found by examining Aleppo and Damascus in Ottoman times.

4.2 Aleppo

Aleppo can serve as an exemplar of a great Levantine city under Ottoman rule. As the capital of a *vilayet*, it enjoyed a strategic site athwart a major trade route to the West, and this was reflected by the presence of permanent European mercantile enterprises, or factories, in the city. While European interest focused on the international textile trade, which embraced both cheap cottons and luxury fabrics woven with gold and silver thread, Aleppo was also the major centre for regional trade, and remained so throughout the Ottoman period. To this day its gigantic covered bazaar, a labyrinth some seven km long, largely an Ottoman creation and perhaps the most impressive in the Arab world, has not degenerated into a tourist trap but is still a living, functioning organism, an entrepôt for hundreds of commodities. Aleppo has remained a mercantile town with its face to the desert. Hence, in part, its prodigious economic vitality, especially in Ottoman times. It was helped in this commercial role not only by its favourable geographical situation, with easy access to the sea, to Anatolia and to Mesopotamia, but also by its large multi-ethnic population. Indeed, in Arab lands it was second in importance only to Cairo, as its large central zone, 10.6 hectares in extent,

testified. The Ottoman period saw a 50 percent increase in this area.

The Ottoman architectural contribution to Aleppo is seen at its most characteristic in the residential quarters (*mahalla*; there were 72 in all) built of high-quality stone masonry. They include far more residences and palaces for the élite than does Jerusalem. The best houses were clustered nearer to the city centre, and were typically between 400 and 900 square metres in ground area, as compared with the 80-190 square metres of the houses built for the middle class and the *haush* system of multiple low houses clustering around a shared courtyard, or on either side of an alley, which—as at Damascus and Jerusalem—was the preferred housing for the urban poor. The standard pattern of élite housing in Aleppo is of an inward-looking structure dominated by a spacious reception room (*qa'a*) and an *iwan* overlooking a courtyard often embellished with a pool, vines and citrus trees. Their decoration draws on local craft traditions which were already well established in the medieval period: inlaid marble in various colours and patterns, and woodwork both carved and painted. This domestic architecture is typified by Bait Jamblat and, in the Judaida quarter, a group of 17th-18th century residences—the Ghazali, Sadir, Ashikbash, Wakil, Balit, Dallal, Sayigh and Basil houses.

In commercial architecture, Aleppo is distinguished by a series of ambitious caravansarais. These include Khan al-Wazir, with its offices ranged around its courtyard, and its monumental portal executed in *ablaq* masonry, Khan al-Nahasin and Khan al-Kattin; some contain mosques, and many are graced with windows whose frames display delicate carving with vegetal and geometric themes. Taken together, these caravansarais underline the scale of the city's trade in Ottoman times. But some have other dimensions too. A *waqf* of Dukaginzade Mehmed Pasha dated 1555 mentions a great mosque, three *khan*s, three *qaisariyya*s and four *suq*s, the whole covering some three hectares. Scarcely less impressive is the Khan al-Gumruk (after 1574), or 'Customs caravansarai', which had two rows of *suq*s adjoining its façade, and with its 344 shops covered an area of 8,000 square metres. But it also lodged the banking houses of the French, English and Dutch, who, following 'capitulation' treaties with the Sublime Porte, had settled in the city from 1562, 1583 and 1613 respectively; here too resided the consuls of these three powers. The Venetians, by contrast, had their own *fondaco* in another quarter. This was the age of the Marseilles merchants and the Levant Company; by 1662 the English factory in Aleppo numbered some fifty traders, and as late as 1775, even in a period of economic decline, there were 80 European firms represented in the city, mainly clustered in the Frankish quarter. Many baths, fountains and workshops for textile manufacture also survive from this period. The domestic and commercial architecture of Ottoman Aleppo is to this day the dominant accent of its urban environment, and is only lightly leavened by buildings of a religious purpose; in that respect, the contrast with Damascus, and even more so Jerusalem, is dramatic. While these vernacular, palatial and mercantile structures are firmly within the local Syrian tradition, the higher-profile public religious architecture in Aleppo, typified by various gubernatorial mosques—the 'Adiliyya (1555), Bahramiyya (1583) and Khusraufiyya (from 1537)—sometimes looked further afield; thus the latter complex, attributed to the court architect Sinan, exhibits close links with the metropolitan architecture of Istanbul.

4.3 Damascus

What of Ottoman Damascus? Like Aleppo, it was a provincial capital; participated in the European trade (for example by exporting the many kinds of damask made by the local women in their homes); had separate quarters for Jews and Christians; and expanded dramatically, especially to the south, as the Maidan suburb shows—indeed, the population doubled in the first three centuries of Ottoman rule. It was in the quarters that the life of the city was concentrated; indeed, Hanafi jurists distinguished between the public and the private zone of a city. These quarters were isolated, a fact symbolised by their being closed at night. The Muslim quarters typically had an oratory, mosque, bath and non-specialised markets, and were thus furnished with all that was needful for community life. Not surprisingly, this sense of closeness had its drawbacks; for example, conflicts between neighbouring quarters were common. Many quarters had a dynamic religious life centred on Sufi brotherhoods, probably because they were close to rural zones. In all these ways Damascus conformed to a pattern that was widespread in the contemporary Near East.

Like Aleppo, it boasted splendid palaces for local notables—for example, the Dahda palace of the 17th century, the house of Nur al-Din, now partially re-erected in the Metropolitan Museum, New York, and dated 1707, or the 'Azm palace of 1749-52, as well as smaller houses of quality like Bait Nizam and Bait Siba'i. Its favourable situation between the intensively cultivated Bika' valley of the Lebanon and the fertile Hauran plateau made it the natural market for central Syria, and it was also the nexus of several arterial routes and a natural entrepôt for the Mediterranean ports.

Like Jerusalem, moreover, its commerce was invigorated by pilgrim traffic—for Damascus, the last major town before the dangerous desert crossing, was a major stage in the *hajj* route. Like Jerusalem, again, it benefited from lavish imperial patronage in the 16th century—notably two *takiya*s, complexes intended *inter alia* to accommodate pilgrims on the *hajj* route. These foundations show how seriously the early Ottoman sultans took the responsibilities attendant upon their honorific title 'Protector of the Two Holy Cities', and thus fit neatly into the pietistic context of early Ottoman architectural patronage in Jerusalem. The *takiya*s are named Salimiyya and Sulaimaniyya after the successive sultans who paid for them; the Salimiyya (1518) was constructed over the tomb of Ibn al-'Arabi, a noted Sufi, which brings to mind the carefully fostered Sufi connections of certain Ottoman sultans. The Sulaimaniyya (1554-5) is the work of the court architect Sinan, who also designed the 'Imarat of Sultan Sulaiman, which was intended for the distribution of food to indigent pilgrims visiting the tomb of Ibn al-'Arabi. Completed in 1552, it is used to this day as a bakery; the parallels with the Khassaki Sultan in Jerusalem are instructive.

Other expressions of government patronage include several *jami's* whose local striped masonry in limestone and basalt is only a veneer for the underlying metropolitan character revealed in such details as hemispherical domes, pencil-shaped minarets and courtyards surrounded by multiple domed bays. Many of the great religious foundations of the Ottoman period were situated outside the city walls, a marked contrast to the situation in Jerusalem and clear proof that Damascus had expanded well beyond its medieval limits. The mosque and mausoleum of Darwish Pasha (1571-5 and 1579 respectively), the Khan al-Harir (1572), also due to him, the mosque of Sinan Pasha (1586-91), the Qaimariyya mosque (1743) built by Fathi Effendi, an official of the Ottoman treasury, the Khan al-Gumruk built by Murad Pasha in 1608-9 and the palace, *madrasa* and *khan* of Asad Pasha al-'Azm all testify to the patronage of enlightened nobles. Well over a dozen Ottoman *khan*s survive; these, unlike so many of the important religious buildings, are *intra muros*. Their size and number clearly reflect the intense commercial activity of Damascus in this period. Only Aleppo among the other cities of the Levant can match this mercantile investment; the almost total absence of such buildings in Ottoman Jerusalem speaks for itself and goes far to explain the much more modest scale of the Ottoman architecture there. The emphasis on tilework in many of the city's Ottoman buildings again brings Jerusalem to mind; Damascus in the 16th and 17th centuries was a thriving centre for the manufacture of glazed ceramics and tiles which are a sub-set of Iznik wares. But Damascus signally lacked stable government. The bare facts are sufficiently telling: between 1516 and 1697 the city was governed by no less than 133 pashas. Few of them did the city much good, for all that the mosque and mausoleum of Darwish Pasha (16th century), and the palace and *khan* of Asad Pasha al-'Azm testify to the patronage of enlightened nobles. It is no accident that the greater prosperity of the city in the 18th century was co-terminous with the tenure of the governorship by members of the 'Azm family for most of that time.

4.4 The local context and pilgrimage

These brief sketches of Ottoman Aleppo and Damascus, which admittedly are biased towards the evidence of the built environment itself, are enough to show that these cities were stylish, sophisticated and metropolitan to a degree that Jerusalem could not match. It is surely significant that when its buildings echo those of Aleppo, Damascus or Cairo—for example the main portal of Khassaki Sultan, with its echoes, as Meinecke has shown, of the *madrasa* of Sulaiman Pasha in Cairo (950/1543-4) and of the tomb of Lutfi Pasha in Damascus (940/1534)—it is precisely because they were the product of exalted patronage. Jerusalem belongs less with these great cities than with, say, Gaza, Hebron, Nablus and Tripoli in this period. For example, in the later 17th century Gaza, then enjoying a period of prosperity, acted as the capital of Palestine, and possessed an attractive set of buildings. As for Hebron, the religious significance conferred on the city by the tombs of the Patriarchs (e.g. Adam, Joseph, and especially Abraham), and the quantity of Muslim pilgrims visiting them—for just as in popular Islam Jerusalem developed as a substitute for Mecca as a pilgrimage destination, so did Hebron develop as a substitute for Madina—ensured that the Ottoman sultans oversaw its upkeep.

Moreover, the route from Damascus to Mecca, followed by some 15,000-20,000 pilgrims every year, and by the supply train for the way back, skirted Jerusalem. Local Beduin chieftains were often appointed to the post of commander of the pilgrimage to Mecca in the 16th and early 17th centuries and they were thus well placed to control Beduin inroads on the *hajj* caravans—for on occasion the pilgrim caravan was almost annihilated by Beduin attacks. The constant need to protect pilgrims (not only those bound for Mecca but also those visiting the shrine of Nabi Musa) meant that the authorities had to raise special troops for this purpose. Clearly the security of the pilgrimage (which obviously had repercussions far outside the local context) was of paramount importance to the Ottoman authorities.

From 1708 the command of the pilgrimage was entrusted to the governor of Damascus, to the economic detriment of Jerusalem—especially since this could involve the imposition of heavy taxation on the pretext of financing the pilgrimage. But despite this setback, the city intermittently played its part in the wider context of Muslim religious life during the Ottoman period.

That said, it is important not to over-estimate the religious role of Jerusalem in the eyes of those who were not natives of the city. The regular pilgrimage route from Damascus by-passed the city. Selim I was the only Ottoman sultan ever to visit the city; even Sulaiman the Magnificent, for all the patronage which he lavished on Jerusalem, and despite the fact that he more than once toyed with the idea of taking a trip there in the course of his frequent visits to Syria, never did so. Kreiser has shown that, while an appointment as *qadi* of Jerusalem was not exactly regarded as a poisoned chalice by ambitious members of the Ottoman *'ulama'*, it was not eagerly sought after. Yet it was emphatically not reserved for local notables; especially during most of the 17th and early 18th century, a substantial majority of the incumbents of this post had held posts in the *madrasa*s of Istanbul. At all events, the position of *qadi* of Jerusalem carried no special cachet in the *cursus honorum* of the Ottoman intellectual hierarchy, and tended to be less of a springboard for future promotion than the final post of an official's career. Even so, the post carried with it not only the prestige of Jerusalem itself but also responsibility for the subsidiary shrines of Hebron and Nabi Musa, and the writ of the Hanafi *qadi* of Jerusalem extended far beyond the borders of the *sanjaq* of Jerusalem.

5 THE ROLE OF THE HARAM IN OTTOMAN TIMES

5.1 The inherent problems of building within the Haram

To build on the Haram al-Sharif—as distinct from building along the outer perimeter of its two terraces—was not a straightforward proposition. It seems probable that there was something of a taboo in operation so far as building within the precinct itself was concerned; hence the very tentative use made of this prime site in post-Umayyad times and even under the Mamluks. On the other hand, the Ottomans were new to Jerusalem and had not been inured to such a taboo. But their readiness to respect the ancient traditions of the site is revealed by their acceptance of the practice, inaugurated at the time of Saladin, that the Maliki imam had pride of place in the timing of the noon and mid-afternoon prayers on the Haram al-Sharif, followed in turn by the Shafi'i, Hanafi and Hanbali imams. This was in spite of the fact that the Ottomans favoured the Hanafi *madhhab*. It is of a piece with this respect for local custom that nothing at all was built in the city in the reign of Selim the Grim (1512-20) and, more to the point, very little in the first fifteen years of the reign of his son and successor, Sulaiman; and when Sulaiman began to build, the Haram had only a minor role in his plans. Two *sabil*s there document this stage of his patronage: Sabil Qasim Pasha (whose inscription exalts him as the Second Solomon) and Sabil Bab al-'Atm. Sabil Qasim Pasha serves for ablutions and is referred to in the *sijill*s as Hanafiyya, in other words it provided the running water which this particular *madhhab* requires for ablution. This proves, incidentally, that not all *sabil*s were built only to furnish drinking water; Sabil Bab al-'Atm, moreover, has a *mihrab* in its north elevation, which serves to mark the *qibla* of an adjoining prayer platform and suggests that it too was intended to serve for ritual ablution. The major new foundations of the new dynasty were the almost neighbouring complexes of Bairam Jawish and Khassaki Sultan, both of them intended to serve Sufis or pilgrims (the former also had a Qur'an school attached to it) and both in the immediate surroundings of the Haram and thus firmly in the Mamluk tradition. Yet both of them are afflicted with a layout that at every turn betrays the acute shortage of space that cramped the architect's design. Indeed, the Khassaki Sultan complex incorporated a hall which was part of the Mamluk foundation of Dar al-Sitt Tunshuq into its design; this was transformed into stables. Clearly there was very little prospect of significant new building activity in this area, where—as noted above—space was at a premium and the detailed provisions of scores of *waqf*s further hampered the free exercise of an architect's imagination. The gap sites were getting smaller all the time. This made it all the more important to extract maximum advantage from them. Thus even a modest little building like the Khalwat al-Dajani is visible from several different angles and is at an important intersection of traffic, while the Khassaki Sultan complex somehow squeezed around its great inner courtyard some fifty-odd rooms with functions as diverse as living quarters for pilgrims, Sufis and travellers, the education of children, storage, worship, communal meals, feeding the poor, stabling, cooking and baking. The Mamluk building boom in Jerusalem, then, had used up practically all the space available for building

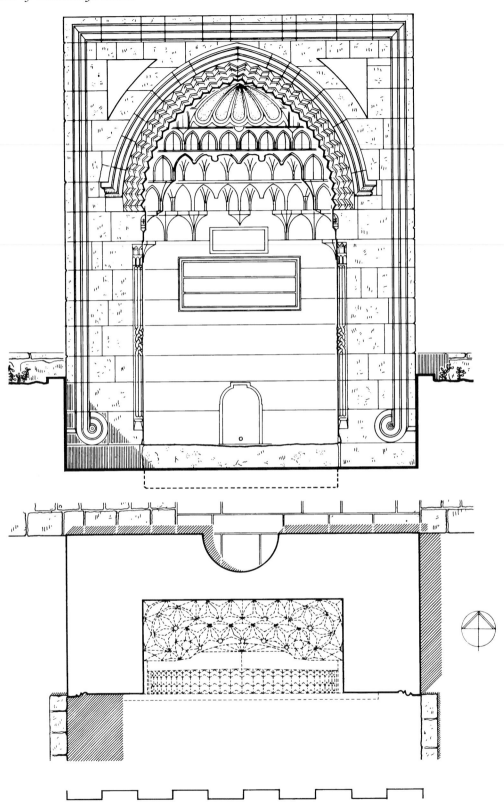

26 Sabil Bab al-'Atm, elevation and plan

immediately outside the western and northern boundaries of the Haram; and the eastern and southern sides had remained unexploited for very good reason—the sheer drop to the south, co-terminous in any case with the city wall itself, and the cemetery area, always taboo for constructions other than funerary ones, to the east. It is noticeable that the only structure built on the eastern side of the terrace is the Ahmadiyya *madrasa*. In view of these constraints, it is not surprising that the decision was taken, however tentatively, to build within the Haram itself. The Mamluks had ensured that their successors had run out of all other options if they were to embellish the Holy City with public religious monuments.

Yet the decision to build within the precincts of the Haram had its own problems. The prestige of the Umayyad monuments was unmatched, for they had the whole weight of Islamic history—including salvation history—behind them. Above all, ample empty space was an essential aspect of the awe-inspiring presence exerted by the Dome of the Rock and the Aqsa Mosque. It was therefore not a serious option to build major new monuments on the Haram and thus to risk upstaging these numinous landmarks. Political considerations also had to be taken into account, for the Ottomans, foreign conquerors whose base was in distant Anatolia right outside the Arabic-speaking world, could not afford to alienate their Arab subjects by intrusive and insensitive construction projects on this immemorially hallowed site. The extent to which, by Ottoman times, the Dome of the Rock and the Aqsa Mosque had come to symbolise the entire city may be gauged by the fact that when the victorious Selim I visited the city in 1516, a group of the *'ulama'* came out of the city to greet him and ceremonially presented him with the keys of these two buildings.

The upshot of all this was that the Ottomans proceeded with extreme circumspection in their development of the Haram area. Even the *sabil*s were located with extreme care—Sabil Bab al-'Atm near the two most conveniently accessible gates on the north side of the Haram, and Sabil Qasim Pasha next to Bab al-Silsila. These were the sole demonstrably Ottoman structures erected on the Haram esplanade in the 16th century, and both were inconspicuously located in the lee of major, much-used gates. *Sabil*s apart, not a single Ottoman sultan, it seems, erected a brand-new structure on the Haram. Given the massive imperial building programme between *c.* 1460 and *c.* 1620, which utterly transformed the face of Istanbul and of numerous cities in Anatolia and the Balkans, this restraint in the third holiest city of the Islamic world is truly remarkable. Yet by slow degrees the Ottomans did contrive to establish their physical presence on the Haram, first on the northern and then on the western side of the upper terrace. The key point to remember is that virtually none of the buildings which did this were imperial. It is symbolic that the first of them, modestly named Hujrat Muhammad after a governor of Jerusalem, was built, probably in 956/1549-50, on the inner northern side of the Haram terrace and was an architecturally insignificant domed square. In its small size, simple form, location and patronage it was prophetic of what was to come. The trickle of such minor, modest buildings never became a flood, but by 1650 or so they permeated the entire precinct. Moreover, quite apart from their impact as individual buildings, they also worked in concert by virtue of the way they clustered together. Thus, taken together, they had modestly and imperceptibly transformed one of the key sites of Islam. Nor should one forget the dimension of sound—prayers could be heard through their open windows and sanctified the entire environment.

5.2 The patronage of Sultan Sulaiman within the Haram

Thus the Ottoman claim to the Haram was staked very modestly and over many decades. This extreme caution brings out the extreme boldness of Sultan Sulaiman's masterstroke, which was nothing short of a *coup de théâtre*: the glamorous refurbishment of the exterior of the Dome of the Rock (colour pls. v, vi, vii, viii, ix, x, xi, xii, xv). It was the perfect way of establishing in visual terms the Ottoman dominion of the city, and the fact that it had come to stay. To any well-travelled contemporary observer, the parallel with the lavish tilework which in these very decades was gracing some of the great mosques of Istanbul itself would have been obvious. Thus the new decoration of the Dome of the Rock, quite apart from its intrinsic splendour, carries the subtext that the building is not just of local importance but has been gathered up into the fold of metropolitan imperial architecture. In rather different language, this visual statement reiterated the political message of the Umayyad caliph 'Abd al-Malik nearly nine hundred years earlier; and it was aimed at the same audience: the people of Jerusalem. But precisely because Jerusalem has for millennia had such wide horizons in religio-political terms, the message of

the second Solomon, broadcast from the site of the first Solomon's Temple, reverberated throughout the Islamic world—and beyond it. The constant flow of pilgrims, Muslims and non-Muslims alike, to Jerusalem would have seen to that. In this context it is worth remembering that the Mamluk historian Mujir al-Din mentions that another king of ancient Israel, this time Hezekiah (who also cut a channel to provide the city with water), constructed six *sabil*s in Jerusalem—a total exceeded only by Sultan Sulaiman. In view of these links with the remote, but living and revered, past it seems tenable to suggest that his own personal name and the immemorial resonances which it bore was itself a factor spurring the sultan to bestow very specific kinds of patronage on Jerusalem. Nor should Sulaiman's desire to be equated with Caesar, with the accompanying implication of continuity between the Roman, Byzantine and Ottoman empires, and the momentous associations of such continuity in contemporary political polemic, be forgotten in this connection. The

27 The Kaiser and Kaiserin Augusta Victoria at the Dome of the Rock in 1898 (American Colony Studio, American Colony Collection)

28 Detail of window-grille, central field, in the Aqsa Museum, Jerusalem

29 Dome of the Rock, octagon window-grille, presumed 10th/16th-century type

30 Dome of the Rock, 10th/16th-century window-grille, formerly in the octagon

31 Dome of the Rock, 10th/16th-century window-grille, formerly in the octagon

32 Dome of the Rock, 10th/16th-century window-grille, formerly in the octagon

whole process began with the transformation of Maqam al-Nabi Da'ud from the Christian shrine commemorating the Last Supper into a mosque in 930/1524. This not only inaugurated the cycle of Sultan Sulaiman's works in Jerusalem but also announced their overall purpose of a public Islamisation of the city.

There is also a strong personal element at work here. As Necipoğlu has shown, the Sulaimaniyya complex at Istanbul, which was built between 1550 and 1557—in other words, at the very same time that this refurbishing was taking place in Jerusalem—contains unmistakable visual echoes of the Dome of the Rock, and in Sulaiman's own mausoleum (the work of his Court Architect, Sinan) at that. The points of resemblance are the external octagon, the double dome, the octagonal ambulatory, the circular colonnade around the central space, and—perhaps most strikingly—the two-tone striped marble voussoirs of the arches above that colonnade. In the decorative scheme they extend to an emphasis on vegetal ornament heightened by jewels (mother-of-pearl in the case of the Dome of the Rock but including rock crystal and actual precious stones in Sulaiman's mausoleum), while the tiles depicting flowers and trees in blossom find a ready parallel in the tilework of the Dome of the Rock. All this is of a piece with the sultan's fondness for quoting Qur'anic passages which mention Solomon and with the references to him in public inscriptions as the Solomon of the Age. The paradisal and Solomonic resonances of Sulaiman's mausoleum were also taken up in the Sulaimaniyya itself. Finally, the mausoleum and the Dome of the Rock share audacious references to the Haram at Mecca itself. A piece of the Black Stone from the Ka'ba was set over the door of the mausoleum and this too has its parallel in Jerusalem, in the black eight-rayed disc so prominently displayed in the lower field of the *mihrab* in the cave under the Rock itself.

Sulaiman's immediate audience, of course, was an Islamic one. He therefore had no need to claim for Islam—as had 'Abd al-Malik—a place of worship long held sacred by other faiths. But he certainly renewed that claim and thus invited comparison with his great Umayyad predecessor. He sought, moreover, to improve on that aspect of the Umayyad achievement which was most obvious to all, namely the colourful exterior mosaic of the building. Especially from a distance, glazed tilework in blue and white (the predominant tones of this composition) has much more visual impact than the more muted palette of mosaic. No evidence has been found to suggest that this mosaic had suffered serious decay. But the history of Islamic architecture is full of examples of later patrons remodelling the decoration of much earlier monuments so as to put their own personal stamp on them. This is what Sulaiman did. It seems unlikely that the good health of the building—or that of the neighbouring Dome of the Chain, which was included in this refurbishment, though a little later, in 1561-2—demanded it. Indeed, he forbore to attempt any major structural intervention. Instead, by sheathing the exterior of the Dome of the Rock in glistening tilework he upstaged his Umayyad predecessor, brought up to date one of the most seminal structures in the Islamic world and established the Ottoman presence right in the middle of the Haram.

This was something that not even the Mamluks had done, despite their sustained embellishment of the Holy City over a period of almost three centuries. They certainly carried out work on the Haram, particularly on its inner façades, and even a certain amount of repair and refurbishing of the Aqsa Mosque and the Dome of the Rock, where the largest single project was Qala'un's repainting of the inner dome. But they attempted nothing so grand and of such public impact as tiling the lower exterior walls of the Dome of the Rock.

It is perhaps a measure of Ottoman imperial pretensions that the project of loading this, the first great monument of Islamic architecture, with redundant ornament should ever have been conceived. It was only the Dome of the Rock that was so singled out, though other buildings in the Haram also benefited from restoration. Thus, while no significant structural work was undertaken at the Aqsa Mosque for almost six centuries after 1350, and indeed it did not offer a comparable opportunity for redecoration, its dome and *qibla* were, according to Evliya Çelebi, both restored under Sulaiman. Scattered references in the *sijills* record further minor running repairs such as the replacement of lead sheeting for the mosque's roof in 996/1588 or the repair of its doors.

It has been suggested that the motive for the redecoration of the Dome of the Rock was a misunderstanding of the themes found in the Umayyad mosaic programme, namely that the depictions of 'cherubim' (probably Sasanian winged motifs) described by Western travellers of the late 15th and early 16th century stimulated an iconoclastic reaction. If so, it was at second hand, for Sulaiman never saw the building, and it seems odd that it took over eight centuries to materialise. Surely it is more likely that the intention was simply to assert the Ottoman presence in Jerusalem by redecorating the city's most celebrated monument. The Sultan's patronage extended, as was the custom, further still—for example to the endowment of Qur'ans and lamps for use in the building. Sulaiman gave the monument a new meaning through the choice of epigraphy: the drum bears Sura 18:1-20 (which refers obliquely to both Christians and Jews) and the date (in figures) 952/1545-6, while lower down the main octagon asserts that the work was carried out by 'the most able masters of their age' and is signed by one 'Abdallah al-Tabrizi, a Persian to judge by his *nisba*, and dated—though there is some dispute about this—959/1551-2. Earlier still, in 935/1528-9, the 36 windows of the outer octagon, whose stucco designs were filled with stained glass, were restored, and presumably this date can be taken, as Meinecke suggests, as marking the start of the entire campaign of refurbishment; the variations in the technique of the tilework point to several distinct campaigns within the overall period. That

period extended over four decades and ended with the installation of bronze-plated doors at the eastern and western entrances to the Dome of the Rock in 972/1564-5; by a pleasing and appropriate symmetry, therefore, it covered almost the entire reign of Sulaiman the Magnificent.

He was also responsible, according to Evliya Çelebi, for the fountain of al-Kas located between the Dome of the Rock and the Aqsa Mosque and approached by 'a meadow over (a pavement of) two hundred paces of white unhewn marble flagstones, laid out by order of Sultan Suleiman'. Al-Kas was a 'huge marble water-basin, made of a single block according to Sultan Suleiman's own directions ... a monument unequalled (for beauty) on earth. It is exquisite and occupies the centre of the platform'. A fragmentary inscription testifies that Sulaiman also restored the north-west colonnade which crowns the steps leading to the upper platform. The stylistic evidence of a distinctive saw-tooth frieze suggests that the Qubbat al-Khadr and substantial parts of the enclosing wall of the Haram around several of the major gates are also of this period. So too, it seems, is the mosque known as Kursi Sulaiman ('The Throne of Solomon') adjoining the east wall of the Haram. Nor should Sulaiman's work on the Citadel be forgotten in this context. The passage of time has blunted the cumulative contemporary impact of this multifarious work of restoration, embellishment and assertion of an Islamic identity in Jerusalem at the behest of the leader of the Sunni world. But in the mid-16th century Jerusalem must have been abuzz with the excitement and perhaps the sense of a special destiny generated by this continuous imperial patronage from the remote capital. Naturally, one effect of all this was to exalt still further the already overwhelming prestige of the Dome of the Rock, a prestige which in Ottoman times found expression in ceremonies of circumambulation *(tawaf)* which excited the disapproval of orthodox theologians like al-Dajani.

For Sulaiman, then, Jerusalem belonged not in a local but in a much wider pietistic context, as already discussed. Most of the major architectural projects of his entire reign were of a religious nature, and they serve to put his works in Jerusalem into context. At his orders the tomb of Abu Hanifa—the founder of the favoured Ottoman *madhhab*—in Baghdad was restored and enlarged; so was the mosque over the tomb of Jalal al-Din Rumi in Konya, an act which publicly affirmed that royal favour for Sufism which was foundational for the Ottoman state. Above all, in Mecca he restored the Ka'ba and the aqueduct, while in Madina he restored the Masjid al-Nabi as well as building walls 12 metres high around the city, with a ditch in front of them. All this building work was clearly consistent with his activities in Jerusalem, and was of a piece with the Ottoman decision to arrogate to the sultan the appointment of the chief *qadi* of Mecca, formerly a privilege of the Grand Sharif of Mecca. Other sacred sites in Palestine also benefited from his patronage. Thus when, in 1552, the domes over the tombs of the patriarchs in Hebron collapsed—they had not been repaired since the time of the Burji Mamluks—orders for their repair were issued from Istanbul. Indeed, a stream of such orders for the repair of the Hebron shrine, together with provisions for creating extra *waqf* property to help with its upkeep and for looking after the stream of pilgrim traffic, and orders for skilled craftsmen to be sent there from Damascus, showed how seriously the Ottoman sultans took their obligations as guardians of the major Islamic shrines. Another example of a shrine that was extensively repaired and enlarged in the Ottoman period is the Maqam of Nabi Musa. It is possible, incidentally, that in undertaking this impressive sequence of pious foundations Sultan Sulaiman may have had it in mind to match the achievements of the Mamluk sultan Qa'it Bay, whose memory would still have been green in the early 16th century and who, besides erecting a *sabil* in the Haram al-Sharif, built aqueducts for Jerusalem; he also erected a *madrasa* adjoining the Masjid al-Haram in Mecca and reconstructed the Masjid al-Nabi in Madina and its domed tomb.

That said, Sulaiman's patronage in Jerusalem pales in comparison with his architectural enterprises in Istanbul—though in both cities there is a notably strong welfare element in his foundations. The absence of any substantial Ottoman *madrasa* in Jerusalem is particularly striking given the role of such foundations in promoting Sunni orthodoxy as interpreted by the Ottoman state.

5.3 Later work on the Haram

The main Ottoman contribution to Jerusalem apart from the walls, the aqueduct and the retiling of the Dome of the Rock is the transformation of the upper terrace of the Haram al-Sharif, on which the Dome of the Rock stands. First the northern and then the western side of this area, the so-called 'inner haram', was embellished. It is important to note from the outset that this transformation was not part of a master plan for the Haram; it happened piecemeal, though the 17th century saw an intensification of this process. This emphasis on the Haram is in such contrast to the trend of almost all Muslim patronage in Jerusalem since Umayyad times that it is worth singling out. Moreover, this commitment to the Haram lasted practically throughout the Ottoman period, even into the 19th century, as the major renovation of that whole area under Sultan Mahmud II in the years 1232-4/1817-19, which involved imported materials and craftsmen from Istanbul and Syria, and the large-scale production of tiles, testifies. Before 1517, the edge of the upper terrace bore only the *minbar* of Burhan al-Din, the colonnades and the Ayyubid Turba al-Nahawiyya. Even before the arrival of the Ottomans, every post-Umayyad structure on the upper terrace was small, discreet and had lots of space around it. This is a sensitive response to the problems of the site and the Ottoman buildings respected this approach, though so far as the sheer number of buildings is concerned theirs is the principal contribution to this palimpsest of piety. It is typical of this respect that the façades of the

The role of the Haram in Ottoman times

33 The Western Mastaba

34 Mastaba to south of the Golden Gate

*hujra*s and similar structures on the upper terrace are uniformly single-storeyed whereas their façades on the lower terrace or esplanade are two- or even three-storeyed. This is a very significant contrast. It meant that, in a most unobtrusive way, these *khalwa*s were able to serve as a bridge between the lower and the upper terrace. The lower floor was also able to profit from using the bedrock, so that there was no need to go to the time and expense of digging foundations. None of the cells have staircases linking the two floors, which underlines the fact that each floor had its own separate function. Understandably enough, the lower and less prestigious floor was reserved for housing indigent pilgrims or Haram staff, and for storage purposes, while the upper level, itself a modest form of self-advertisement on the part of the patron, functioned as a place of worship and study (perhaps also as a dormitory) for Sufis, and was often further dignified by a vaulted porch which could serve similar purposes without encroaching too obviously on the open space of the Haram. As Evliya Çelebi notes, these cells were occupied by 'pious people considered to be the wonder-working Dervishes. Some of them break their fast only once a week, while others may not have tasted meat for forty or fifty years'. As late as the 19th century Wilson notes that these cells had 'Underground rooms [he no doubt meant their lower level] . . . for destitute Muslim pilgrims who ate and slept at the Mosque's expense', and

Catherwood, writing a little earlier, notes that 'one portion of these [cells] is devoted to the black pilgrims from Africa'. Thus the welfare network which was an integral part of the ritual of pilgrimage to Jerusalem continued right up to modern times.

5.4 Methods of sanctifying the Haram

Several other ways of sanctifying the Haram are worth brief mention here. The *mastaba*—a very slightly raised platform used for open-air prayer—helped assert a presence on the Haram without breaking up the familiar view (colour pl. xxvi). The finial of most of the cells and aedicules on the Haram is Mecca-oriented, another (if understated) way of emphasising their religious function, while the Iwan al-Sultan Mahmud II (colour pl. xxii) is aligned to the Dome of the Rock. More distantly, high-rise buildings located relatively far from the Haram might nonetheless be designed to offer sight-lines to its monuments. Thus a view of the Dome of the Rock can be enjoyed from the Zawiya al-Muhammadiyya, though from its side chambers rather than the main ones.

It is worth reflecting briefly on the nature of these Ottoman structures. It is hard to interpret a single one of them as justified by an imperative religious, social or public need. In any event, their tiny size would have militated against their performing any such function. By and large, these are not buildings erected for the public good. Once again, one sees Ottoman patrons paying the price of arriving too late on a site already hallowed by Islam for almost a millennium. One suspects that some of these cells reflect a low-key competition among minor Ottoman functionaries for a place—any place—on the Haram. After all, some 60 percent of the Ottoman buildings in the city are concentrated there, and this trend accelerated markedly in the last two and a half centuries of Ottoman rule.

All this is not to deny that these cells do serve a wider purpose in the architecture of the Haram. Their location shows a consistent desire to line the perimeter of the upper terrace—the prime focus of Ottoman building activity—with minor monuments. They form a kind of *cordon sanitaire*. The Kursi Sulaiman, strategically placed at the north-east corner of the Haram, seems to express the same idea. It remains an open question whether the parcelling out of the available lots on the site was governed by any hierarchy or notion of privilege. Perhaps this might explain why the west and north sides were built up rather more heavily than the east side, which is largely empty to this day. Fifteen cells were built around the west, north and east sides of the upper terrace of the Dome of the Rock. Four of these are of a higher standard than almost all the rest (North-western and North-eastern Khalwas of Ahmad Pasha, his *madrasa*, and Khalwa al-Junbalatiyya). They are the work of one patron and one decade and probably one local architect: ʿAbd al-Muhsin b. Mahmud b. Nammar, who was probably also responsible for Hujrat Islam Beg (colour pls. xiv and xvi) and Khalwat Bairam Pasha. The family produced at least five generations of architects and thirteen of the seventeen holders of the prestigious post of *miʿmarbashi* (Chief Architect) in the 16th and 17th centuries belonged to it. Their status was underlined by the use of

titles with the elements *ʿain* (source) and *fakhr* (pride), and one may perhaps assume that their importance found expression in the particular buildings with which they were most concerned. Certainly the lower terrace contains far fewer minor buildings than does the upper terrace, and a difference in status between the two areas seems a possible explanation.

What, then, were the options open to the Ottomans as successors to the Mamluks and guardians of Islam's third holiest city? It must be conceded that they were unpalatably limited. After all, as already explained, the immediate surroundings of the Haram were already crammed with impressive Mamluk monuments and there was no obvious area in the most prestigious part of the city in which an Ottoman enclave could be built from scratch. True, much of the Haram was empty; but, as already noted, that emptiness was a necessary element of its design and function. Thus the Haram was indeed available, but only for small-scale structures; and such buildings necessarily sent out a somewhat modest message. It is scarcely surprising that the patronage which produced them was not royal.

It might be argued that, for all their modest size, these buildings could have had more impact had their decoration been more lavish. After all, there was the possibility of spectacular colour in the Ottoman even more than in the Mamluk architecture of Jerusalem because, added to the wide choice of coloured stone, for example yellow, red and pink stone, was the option of technicolour tilework. Yet this option was scarcely used, except in the case of the Dome of the Rock. Polychromy in stone was indeed used, but only very sparingly, which again points to the modest ambitions if not also the modest means of the patrons. Moreover, the Ottoman architectural style did not favour applied ornament, in contrast to the Mamluk style which virtually depended on it. Thus there was no way that the Ottomans could have outdone Mamluk patronage by fancy decoration; they would simply have had to build on a much larger

35 Muslim religious dignitaries standing outside the Khalidi Library, Jerusalem (Collection of Eric Matson, Library of Congress, Washington, DC)

36 Sabil Tariq al–Wad, 943/1536 (photo Joe Rock)

37 Sabil Birkat al-Sultan

scale; and even if the money had been available to do this, it is a moot point whether the tiny population of the city could have justified such expense.

5.5 The Haram: pilgrimage and scholarship

The role of the Haram as a magnet for pilgrims needs to be taken into account. Nasir al-Din Rumi, writing in the mid-16th century, makes it clear that there is a set itinerary for the Muslim pilgrim to the holy places in Jerusalem. Perhaps the most famous guide to the Holy Places—Mecca, Madina and Jerusalem—is the *Dala'il al-Khairat* of the Berber mystic al-Jazuli (d. 869/ 1465), which, with much other material such as prayers for the Prophet, outlines these itineraries. Illustrated copies of this work with detailed views of the three Holy Cities became very popular in Ottoman times. Thus a list of key religious sites was easily available, and was often used by those seeking to acquire merit by such pious visitations, and by those paying for pilgrimage by proxy (colour pl. i). The parallel with the Stations of the Cross is striking.

It should be noted, however, that topographical accuracy was not a major aim of these guides and certificates; instead, they gradually perfected an abstract visual language of their own which was well suited to suggesting an other-worldly reality (colour pls. iii and iv). In these works the Dome of the Rock may be depicted in elevation, in plan, or in both at once. In plan it may be rendered as circular or as an uneven octagon, with shorter sides on the diagonals. Similarly, the Haram al-Sharif has its perimeter picturesquely but erroneously adorned with a quartet of cypress trees or of Ottoman-style minarets, and the upper terrace may be depicted not as rectangular but with ten or even seventeen sides. As for the Aqsa Mosque, the 7-bay façade which it had had probably since Fatimid times is reduced to five bays or less, sometimes with

a powerfully salient porch, secondary domes or arcades in two tiers. All this is clearly fantasy architecture. As for the lack of consistency in these representations, this feature finds an arresting parallel in the sequence of 38 Ottoman tiles listed by Erdmann, largely of the 17th century and depicting the Ka'ba. He suggests that these minor differences can be explained either by the desire of patrons who were *hajji*s to inject an element of personal observation into a stereotypical image or by the sheer variety of illustrated guidebooks that were available.

Even images that attempt a much more representational manner—'realism' would be quite the wrong word here—present the entire Haram al-Sharif according to a schema which is, so to speak, unnecessarily inaccurate. Thus the *Falnama* of Shah Tahmasp, in a scene of dervishes engaged in prayer and meditation around the Dome of the Rock while one of their number, half-naked, clings to its door like Majnun at the Ka'ba, creates an ambience which conveys a generalised sanctity rather than the sense of a specific place (colour pl. ii). The central domed structure is hexagonal while its open precinct is octagonal and defined by continuously crenellated arcades regularly punctuated by minarets of Ottoman type, six in all. One might be inclined to doubt that the Haram al-Sharif is the intended subject here; but, as Bernardini has pointed out, a nearby illustration in the same manuscript depicts the Prophet's sandals, whose imprint within the Dome of the Rock was the focus of pious visitation in Jerusalem during the Ottoman period (colour pl. iv, left) and perhaps owed something to an older cult of veneration centred on the footprints of Jesus. The briefest study of medieval renderings of the Dome of the Rock—for example in the Edinburgh manuscript of al-Biruni's *al-Athar al-Baqiyya* of 707/ 1307-8 or the Paris manuscript of al-Qazwini's *'Aja'ib al-Makhluqat* of 790/1388—suffices to indicate that there was no widely accepted pictorial convention for depicting it.

Nor should the allure of Jerusalem for religious scholars—such as al-Khiyari, al-Nabulsi, al-Siddiqi, al-Zayyani and al-Luqaimi, whose accounts have been analysed by Rafeq among others—be forgotten. Throughout the Ottoman centuries there was a steady stream of visitors from all over the Arab world in particular—from Arabia, Syria, Egypt and North Africa. Many came to study with local scholars, exchanging visits with them, debating with them, attending their classes and also giving lessons or issuing *ijaza*s; some, especially Malikis, settled in the city for long periods; and still others came to visit the major religious buildings, notably the Dome of the Rock and the Aqsa Mosque, sometimes taking the opportunity to pray with different imams there, visiting or staying in Sufi establishments or paying their respects at shrines and at the tombs of the illustrious dead. Sites of Christian and Jewish significance were also visited, for example by al-Nabulsi. These various motives for visiting the Holy City were of course not mutually exclusive. The Sufi presence in Ottoman Jerusalem was much stronger than the tally of surviving buildings might suggest—the Muslim travellers record several Sufi foundations which have long vanished—and at times found very public expression in the visitation of shrines to the accompaniment of the beating of drums and the waving of banners. The similarities in the accounts left by such travellers indicate that those in charge of showing visitors around the principal buildings had a fairly standard body of information to impart, with a strong emphasis on symbolic exegesis of architectural features such as the 17 types of marble to be found in the *mihrab* of the Aqsa Mosque. The frequent references to the works of Mujir al-Din and al-Suyuti indicate that these were the standard guidebooks for the monuments of Jerusalem.

5.6 The economic role of the Haram

Finally, one must consider the economic role of the Haram al-Sharif in the life of the city. In a survey of 120 documents dealing with shops, Salameh

discovered that no less than 78 of them were endowed to the Haram al-Sharif, a vivid illustration of the central role which the Haram played in the society of Ottoman Jerusalem—for the rents of these shops varied from two and a half to nine hundred silver *halabi*s a month depending on their location. When this economic preponderance of Haram-controlled commercial property is placed in the wider context of all the other *madrasa*s, houses, other properties and land which had also been made *waqf* in favour of the Haram, it could be said that the history of the city is the history of its endowments.

Other aspects of the economic impact of the Haram should also not be forgotten. Like many shrines and religious complexes throughout the Islamic world, it was a major employer. This was especially the case so far as its dependent *madrasa*s were concerned (though they formed separate units from the economic point of view, since their endowments were of very unequal value, and this was a factor in renting some of them out for residential use). Some of the posts in these *madrasa*s could be inherited, and they were regularly bought and sold. At what might be called the professional level, the Haram had a steady requirement for religious scholars to teach in these *madrasa*s, of *shaikh*s to run them, of imams, preachers and inspectors, of all kinds of administrators and trustees for its many *waqf*s, of Qur'an readers to recite in the many *khalwa*s as well as in the Dome of the Rock and the Aqsa Mosque, reciters of *hadith* (for example the *Sahih* of al-Bukhari), of scribes, *qadi*s, muezzins and tax collectors. Qur'an reciters in particular required a licence, and many *waqf*s specified one reciter per *juz'*, so that as many as 33 readers—presumably for a 30-*juz'* Qur'an—were appointed; and they had the right to arrange for substitutes to take their place, thus enlarging the employment pool still further—though many cases are recorded of men who held more than one post at a time. Salameh cites the example of the *qadi* Sa'd al-Din ibn al-Muhandis, who held jobs in at least five *madrasa*s besides holding a licence to act as *shaikh* and water-carrier in the Madrasa al-Salahiyya and eventually becoming its inspector. He was also *shaikh* of the Jauhariyya Khanqah while at the Ghadariyya Madrasa he was imam, reciter and doorkeeper. The combination of posts which he held at both the Ghadariyya and the Salahiyya Madrasas present an odd juxtaposition of lofty and menial responsibilities. It is not hard to imagine the inherent conflicts of interest in such arrangements, and not surprisingly

Sa'd al-Din was challenged in successive court cases; but he battled tenaciously for the right to hold his positions. A small army of workers in more humble occupations was also needed: lamp-lighters, doormen, carpet-spreaders, sweepers, janitors and water carriers. No doubt the cachet of working for one of the major shrines in the entire Islamic community was an extra inducement to apply for such jobs.

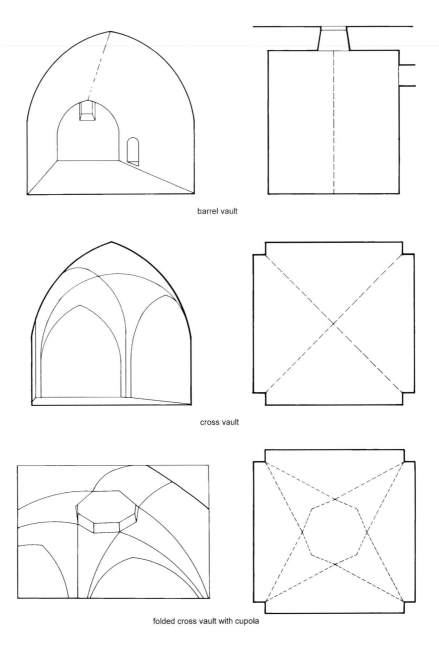

barrel vault

cross vault

38 Vault types   folded cross vault with cupola

52

6 THE NATURE OF OTTOMAN PATRONAGE IN JERUSALEM

6.1 Imperial patronage

There is an obvious distinction to be made between royal and local patronage. To the first category belong the walls, the aqueduct, canals and pools, the re-tiling of the Dome of the Rock, the *sabil*s and the Khassaki Sultan. With the exception of the *sabil*s—which though beautiful enough in all conscience, and undeniably Islamic, are cheap—these all represent major financial investments in the city. All of them, moreover, the *sabil*s included, are high-profile enterprises; they affected directly the daily life of every citizen of Jerusalem. The aqueduct and its associated facilities brought clean water within reach of everyone; the walls and the rebuilt Citadel assured the security of the whole population; the re-tiling of the Dome of the Rock could have been seen as a lavish gesture to honour the city's most famous and charismatic monument; and the Khassaki Sultan complex (like its eponymous counterpart in Istanbul, datable to 1536, which also fitted into a gap site and is also still functioning) was *inter alia* a massive welfare project targeting the poorest members of society. The sheer scale of that project is graphically reflected in several ways apart from the surface area of this congeries of buildings—in the fact that at one stage it was consuming half of the available water in the city, in the size of the cauldrons from Khassaki Sultan, which are preserved in the Haram museum, and, more to the point, in the fact that the income from villages scattered over five *sanjaq*s (Jerusalem, Gaza, Nablus, Safad and Sidon) was required for its operations. No more extensive charitable complex was ever built by the Ottomans in Palestine, and the size of its *waqf*s was exceeded

only by those for the Haram itself. All this is patronage on a grand scale. Its hallmark is vision.

How is one to interpret this continuous enterprise? Since all of these works were carried out within the space of half a generation, their cumulative effect is hard to exaggerate. They far outshone any single Mamluk contribution to the embellishment of Jerusalem, and seem to lack that element of direct personal self-interest that marks so many medieval Islamic charitable foundations. They illustrate a type of patronage distinctively different from that of the Mamluks, for they are aimed at society at large rather than at a small segment of it—those people who would, for example, benefit from a *ribat*, *madrasa* or *khanqah*. Most Mamluk patronage was of this piecemeal, more specialised kind, although it did consistently lean towards private charitable institutions. Naturally there are exceptions: the work of Sultan Hasan in rebuilding the north-east part of the Aqsa Mosque and of Sultan al-Malik al-Nasir Muhammad on Suq al-Qattanin, do have wider perspectives. But even so, there are only three royal Mamluk foundations in Jerusalem to commemorate that dynasty's 267 years of power in the city—a striking contrast to the magnificent output of the Ottoman sultans (especially Sulaiman) in the first half-century of their tenure. Ottoman patronage, moreover, is different from that of the Mamluks in other ways too. It smacks of a plan drawn up in Istanbul rather than one worked out on the spot. This patronage at arm's length, so to speak, makes it unlikely that Sulaiman was actuated by a desire to match the patronage of the Mamluks in Jerusalem, or at least to continue their work. Enough has been said to indicate that royal Ottoman patronage fostered to a degree unprecedented in Islamic Jerusalem both the practical

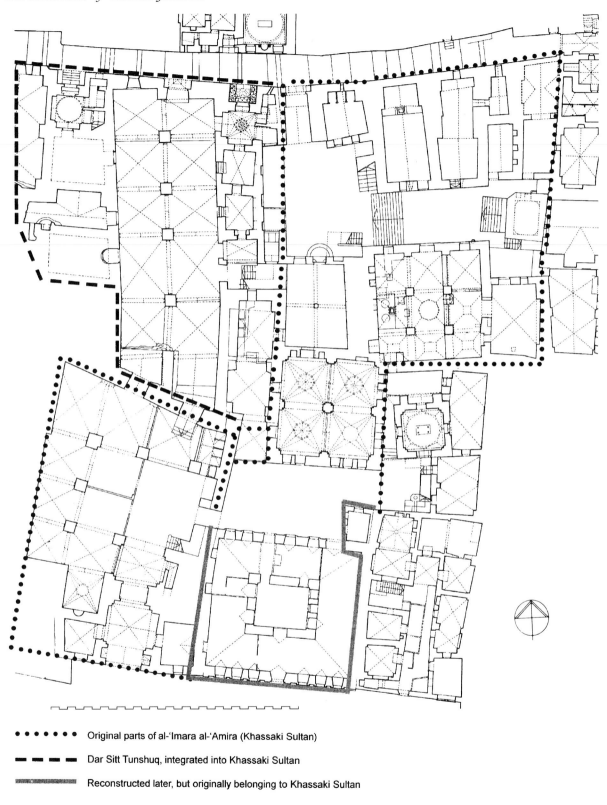

●●●●●●● Original parts of al-ʻImara al-ʻAmira (Khassaki Sultan)

━ ━ ━ ━   Dar Sitt Tunshuq, integrated into Khassaki Sultan

▨▨▨▨▨   Reconstructed later, but originally belonging to Khassaki Sultan

39 Al-ʻImara al-ʻAmira (Khassaki Sultan), overall ground plan

40 Al-'Imara al-'Amira (Khassaki Sultan), aerial photograph showing the complex in context. 'Aqabat al-Takiyya is to the right of the photograph, 'Aqabat al-Saraya to the left.

41 Al-'Imara al-'Amira (Khassaki Sultan), south façade of complex along 'Aqabat al-Sarayya

42 Al-'Imara al-'Amira (Khassaki Sultan), outer wall along 'Aqabat al-Takiyya

55

daily welfare of its people and their lively sense of the special destiny of their city. He was its last and greatest patron—greater even than the Umayyad caliph 'Abd al-Malik—and yet he never set foot in it. Moreover, his interest in the city spanned almost his entire reign, from the Sabil al-Mahkama of 1527 to the refurbishment of the Dome of the Chain in 969/ 1561-2—for which, as Meinecke suggests, the team of tilework specialists who had recently completed the embellishment of the *takiya* of Sultan Sulaiman at Damascus in 967/1560 was probably responsible. No later Ottoman sultan achieved very much in the way of architectural patronage in Jerusalem, and this too highlights the scale of his work there.

Yet, as already noted above, this undeniably impressive achievement is dwarfed by the scale of his foundations in Istanbul itself, notably the gigantic *külliye* named after him, of which the mosque is the core, half-a-dozen other large mosques, several *madrasa*s and—as at Jerusalem— the reconstruction of the water system. The fact that no major new mosque was built in Jerusalem by any Ottoman sultan, while in Istanbul a whole series of them, monuments of world stature, was erected in the 16th century, speaks for itself. Nor was it a matter of new mosques being confined to Istanbul; Cairo, for example, saw several major foundations in this period, such as the mosques of Sinan Pasha (1571) and Malika Safiyya (1610), to say nothing of literally hundreds of smaller buildings, including scores of *sabil-kuttab*s. In fact, this type of monument—unknown in Ottoman Jerusalem, with the possible exception of the Khassaki Sultan—was almost a trademark of Ottoman Cairo; 50 of the 63 Ottoman *sabil*s in Cairo have a *kuttab* or *maktab* in the upper floor, which comprises a single chamber. Jerusalem, it is true, preserves five minarets of Ottoman date; but these are notably unadventurous. Their stumpy cylinders, articulated by balconies carried on *muqarnas* corbels, rest on chamfered bases. Relatively crude in structure and decoration, they are a poor substitute for major mosques, especially as none of them rival the slender, elegant spires of the Ottoman capital. They do, however, serve— thanks to their carefully chosen sites—to assert the Islamic presence in the city, a theme announced at the very outset of Ottoman rule in the transformation of the Christian Coenaculum, the supposed site of the Last Supper, into Maqam al-Nabi Da'ud. This too has its Ottoman minaret. A related propaganda purpose may be inferred from the presence of an Ottoman minaret in the Citadel.

One other element of royal patronage in Jerusalem requires brief mention here, and it points in the same direction as the remarks in the previous paragraph. It is the emphasis on the re-use and reworking of existing buildings. The list is long: the Damascus Gate, the Dome of the Rock and the Dome of the Chain, the Sitt Tunshuq complex, the Church of St Agnes, and the Coenaculum all come readily to mind, and there are lesser instances too. Such re-use or re-working, which very often involves changes of function, is a way of stamping the royal presence on the pre-existing urban fabric and is thus another form of appropriation, admittedly less grand in its impact than were the walls or the rebuilt Citadel. But the main point here is that, by and large, such re-shaping is much cheaper than building from scratch.

In assessing the architecture of Ottoman Jerusalem synoptically, it is instructive to consider not only what was built but also what was not built. That must be done with care, and with a full consciousness that Jerusalem was not a great Ottoman city of the likes of Aleppo or Damascus, let alone Cairo or Istanbul itself. One might argue that it did not have the population to sustain great buildings—though its earlier Islamic history, whether in remote Umayyad times or in the recent Mamluk past, suggests otherwise, or at any rate suggests that population was by no means the only factor. Thus the propaganda element never far removed from the public architecture of this city must be taken into account. With these provisos in mind, one may turn to the problem of what is not there in the corpus of Ottoman architecture in Jerusalem.

By far the most important absence is an imperial mosque. It is surely very odd that Sultan Sulaiman, having spent so much on the walls and on the Dome of the Rock, spent nothing on the Aqsa Mosque. The absence of a brand-new great imperial mosque is not, however, hard to explain, for outside the Haramain—where Sulaiman was also an active patron—there is no congregational mosque in the Islamic world of greater sanctity than the Aqsa Mosque. Its size was such that it easily served the needs of the Muslims of the city. But it remains odd that no major refurbishment of its fabric was undertaken.

Other omissions are scarcely less strange. Sulaiman founded no *külliye*, although that was a favoured building type in the imperial capital. The nearest approach to such a complex is the 'Imarat Khassaki Sultan, which was financed not by the sultan himself but by his wife. There was not one large *madrasa*, although such foundations were an essential of the Ottoman *cursus honorum*. Similarly, there were no large *khans* despite the huge pilgrim traffic to the city and the Ottoman penchant for building spacious urban *khans*, of which there are many which still survive in Damascus and Aleppo.

6.2 Local patronage

Local patronage in Jerusalem was of course a much more modest affair. Indeed, anonymous patronage was virtuous according to some religious teaching. But whether the patrons were named or not, the critical factor was, as ever, not a sudden drop in the capacities of the craftsmen, but in the amount of cash available for building activities. After *c.*1600 political and economic decline, which had set in after the death of Sulaiman the Magnificent, accelerated, and restricted still further the scope of architectural patronage. But even so, in the previous century the absence of foundations by Sinan, the Chief Architect (*mi'marbashi*) to the Ottoman court from 1538 to 1588, is marked, especially as his work is so widely found in the

Ottoman provinces. The report by Evliya Çelebi, in his account of Sulaiman's dream in which the Prophet urged him to rebuild Jerusalem, that Sinan was despatched to Jerusalem to carry out the work, is not borne out by any other testimony; there is, for example, no mention of this in the *sijill*s. The same goes for Evliya's assertion that the tiled inscription band on the drum of the Dome of the Rock was designed by the premier Ottoman calligrapher Ahmad Qarahisari. In the case of non-royal foundations there is no evidence of strict control imposed from Istanbul. Most of the buildings of Ottoman Jerusalem were built by local men for local patrons. Indeed, in the 16th century governors accounted for twelve of the buildings erected as against the nine erected at the behest of the sultans themselves, though it must be conceded that gubernatorial patronage was on a much more modest scale. As for the later Ottoman period (1010-1247/1601-1831), the patronage of the governors account for nineteen buildings and that of the sultans for ten. The trend is therefore clear. Unidentified patrons erected seven buildings in the first period and fourteen in the second.

It is important not to be misled by these numbers. The central fact is that with the death of Sulaiman the Magnificent in 1566, Jerusalem ceased to bulk large in the consciousness of the Ottoman sultans, and the patronage of local governors was a sorry substitute for that of royalty. The city was given by the Ottoman authorities to its successive governors as a tax farm, and since their term of office was often no longer than two or three years, they had a strong incentive to make as much money out of the post as possible before relinquishing it. This was emphatically not a situation which encouraged such men to spend their money on public works. Similarly, in Ottoman Cairo the brief tenure of office allotted to the Turkish governors discouraged them from erecting major buildings. To judge by the wording of the relevant *waqfiyya*s, a significant motive in these foundations is embodied in their quotations from the Qur'an, such as 'On the Day whereon neither wealth nor sons will avail, but only he (will prosper) that brings to Allah a sound heart' (Sura 26: 88-9) or from the *hadith*: 'When a man dies, all his works cease, except for three things: an ongoing act of charity, some learning which gives benefit, and a pious son who will pray for him.'

Given the large quantity of buildings erected in Jerusalem in the first eighty years of Ottoman suzerainty, it is striking that only five were built outside the Haram between 1600 and 1831, and those comprised two *zawiya*s, two *sabil*s and the Dar al-'Izz—in other words, nothing ambitious. This is indeed a telling illustration of the gradual decline in the city's fortunes over this long period.

6.3 Bairam Jawish

In Jerusalem, the major exception to the trend favouring small structures are the foundations of Bairam Jawish. They have the further distinction of being concentrated in a limited area, namely Tariq 'Aqabat al-Takiyya. This street had already

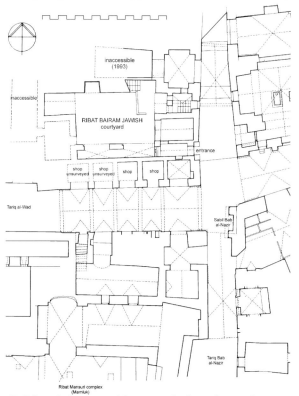

43 Ribat Bairam Jawish, ground plan of complex

been used as a site for major foundations in Mamluk times, and Bairam Jawish was forced to shoehorn his new buildings into the limited and irregular space available. But he went even further than this by acquiring a ruined building on a corner site—particularly coveted because it allowed the maximum number of passers-by to hear the sound of Qur'anic recitation for the benefit of the tenant of the tomb, and to participate in that recitation. He promptly renovated this structure to form a *maktab*. This follows a familiar Mamluk pattern in that its prime function was not its ostensible one—i.e. a school for orphans—but to act a burial place for Bairam Jawish (preferably as close as possible to the Haram?), and the eastern chamber of the ground floor is given over to this purpose. Thus anyone entering the building could not have failed to notice the founder's tomb. But this tomb is not a self-contained structure; it is merely a cross-vaulted lower room in a much larger structure. Thus the Mamluk obsession with massive mausolea has diminished. But it remains a problem as to how children were taught in the context of this building, how big the classes were, and what age groups were catered for here. The simplicity of the facilities—essentially a succession of large halls or chambers—would lend itself to multiple uses. Perhaps this was indeed the original intention. Bairam Jawish was the administrator in charge of the neighbouring Khassaki Sultan, and thus he lived 'above the shop'. He would therefore have been well placed to oversee how his own foundation was being used. The details of the *waqf* which he set up for this complex of buildings, as recorded in the *sijill*s, constitute the longest such document known in Ottoman Jerusalem apart from that for Khassaki Sultan. Nearby was his own house (colour pl. xviii), built in 959/1551-2 and graced with a view of the Dome of the Rock thanks to its location well above street level. The building activities of Bairam Jawish, complemented by those of Sulaiman's consort Hürrem, made the Tariq 'Aqabat al-Takiyya the major focus of Ottoman patronage in Jerusalem after the Haram itself.

6.4 *Waqf*

The standard method of securing the future for a charitable foundation was, as it had been for many centuries, the pious endowment or *waqf*. Although the central government supported the Aqsa Mosque and several other buildings (such as Kursi Sulaiman) by a sum *(al-surra)* sent annually to Jerusalem from Istanbul, the number of major public *waqf*s under the Ottomans was remarkably limited—those of Khassaki Sultan, the As'adiyya Zawiya and Maqam al-Nabi Da'ud. Thus most *waqf*s are private, and partially-owned property plays a major role in these endowments. Many of the best-documented *waqf*s are those of the traditional Jerusalem families, which represent some 21 percent of the Muslim *waqf*s registered in the *sijill*s of the Shari'a Court between 1514 and 1919 (about a quarter of the 2,128 *waqf*s registered in this period in the *sijill*s are Christian and Jewish). These endowments registered by members of the traditional local families seem to have been used primarily for private as distinct from public and charitable purposes, as the researches of Dr Mohammad 'Alami indicate; they served to retain and concentrate wealth and benefits in kind in the family of the testator, especially his male descendants. The evidence of the *sijill*s suggests that most *waqf*s are of modest value because of their limited economic base which itself is in no small measure due to the fragmented nature of property ownership noted above; but there is little doubt that a combination of individually small endowments could nonetheless add up to a respectable rental income. Even so, and notwithstanding the exceptional public *waqf*s mentioned above (notably the Khassaki Sultan complex), the sad truth is that the end of Mamluk power also spelt the end of substantial endowments for the buildings of Jerusalem. Furthermore, much of the income on which the functioning and maintenance of religious monuments in Jerusalem depended in the Ottoman period came from *waqf*s which had been established in Mamluk times.

The *sijill*s, besides being crammed with information which bears on the operation of individual *waqf*s, also contain more than a score of complete or incomplete *waqfiyya*s, and these provide a treasury of detail. A few specific examples will reveal something of how the system worked. Thus the *waqf* of Bairam Jawish for his *ribat* (which functioned as a hospice for the poor) and *maktab* (here, a school for orphans) was originally registered in Gaza, even though it referred to a property in Jerusalem. Much of the *waqf* property in this case was located in Bethlehem. If Bairam Jawish's family died out, the endowment stipulated that the Inspector of his *waqf* was to be the Nazir al-Haramain al-Sharifain (i.e. superintendent of the Aqsa and Hebron sanctuaries). In this particular case, the rate of interest charged on the capital sum was 15 percent. This rate continued for another generation; the *waqf* of the Hujra of Islam Beg, dated 1002/1593-4, was a capital sum of 500 gold *sultani*s, to be administered so as to yield a legal profit of 75 (i.e. 15 percent); the *mutawalli* was to avoid usury *(riba)*. The money was to go on administration and on seven reciters of the Qur'an (the benefit of the readings and associated prayers was to go to the founder, his brother, the founder's family and all deceased Muslims). About a century later, Yusuf Pasha made a *waqf* of 95 *ghirsh as'adi* (gold coins) to pay for two reciters in the Dome of the Rock, oil to illuminate the cave of the Dome of the Rock and for people in charge of lighting the lamp, and for the administrator of this *waqf*; the annual amount was to be 14 and one third *ghirsh*, i.e. about 15 percent. Soon after, however, in 1665-6, *waqf* money was attracting interest at the standard rate for all transactions: an extortionate 20 percent, as the case of the Khanqah al-Maulawiyya shows. Here part of the original capital had been lost in the course of successive administrations. The running costs of this building were met in that year by the income from two houses, a single room, a stable, three chambers, a storage place, and a plot of land—all in the Maulawiyya complex or nearby. The *waqf* of the Sabil al-Khalidi is typical in the scrupulous care with

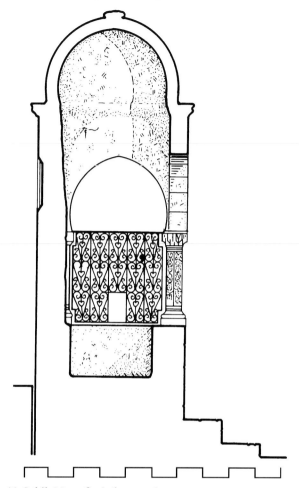

44 Sabil Mustafa Agha, section

45 Sabil Mustafa Agha, south-west corner column

which it defines the exact site of the building to be endowed; indeed, the setting for this vanished *sabil* has scarcely changed to this day from what it was in the early 18th century. Another *waqf* for the Khanqah al-Maulawiyya specifies 3 kg of bread and 6 kg of meat (presumably provided daily?) and a reduction of the allowance to 1,470 piastres a month to feed all members of the order. The *waqf* of the North-western Khalwa of Ahmad Pasha specifies that some of the money should be set aside for oil for the lamp (this is a common provision in the *waqf*s of Jerusalem) and for restoring the doors of the building. The *waqf* of the Qubbat al-Arwah, too—an open-plan aedicule in the middle of the largely empty upper terrace of the Haram (colour pl. xv)—provides for a lamp to be lit throughout the hours of darkness, though the purpose of this provision is

not specified. The *waqf* of the Khalwat Bairam Pasha mentions that *qusurmil* (building material) was provided for the monument, while that of the Zawiya al-Muhammadiyya covered such unusual annual expenses as mats for the floor of the *zawiya* and posts to support the trellis of the grapevine over the main entrance and south wall of the *zawiya*. In other cases cash in the form of direct salaries, grants and stipends predominated. Thus the *waqf* of the Madrasa of Ahmad Pasha states that the teacher *(mudarris)* will have a salary of 500 silver *misriyya* per year, and each of the four students a stipend of 50 silver *misriyya* per year. Teacher and students were to pray for the patron and his ancestors. The Sabil of Mustafa Agha (colour pl. xxviii) had a *waqf* of 40 gold coins, and the caretaker was allotted four gold coins annually, to be paid so long as this capital sum remained intact. In some cases cash and kind were combined. For instance, a *waqf* of 1038/1628-9 for

46 Al-Zawiya al-Muhammadiyya, external street façade with domes

the Hujra of Muhammad Agha provided money for a Qur'an reader who every morning was to recite Sura 36 (Ya Sin) in the upper part of the *hujra*; the merit of the reading was for the soul of the Prophet Muhammad. For this he got 12 gold pieces a year, plus permission to live in the lower part of the building and to profit from cultivating the small garden attached to the *hujra*. Similarly, the *waqf* of the Sabil al-Shurbaji, which was based on the income from three and a half shops, paid for two people to run the *sabil*: a caretaker to keep it clean and illumine it during Ramadan and Sha'ban, and a water-carrier; while the *waqf* of the Odat Arslan Pasha stipulates that the reader has to recite the Qur'an and the normal petitions plus prayers to the Prophet and invocations to Allah. It has to be admitted, however, that the *waqf* system was frequently manipulated to pay the salaries of redundant officials.

The *waqf* of al-Zawiya al-Naqshbandiyya is one of the more interesting and informative examples and shows how a *waqf* could be rooted in the local neighbourhood and affect the local economy. It provides for only four members of the order to be housed in that building, and by the second half of the 19th century it was serving the Jerusalem poor with accommodation and food. Half of the *waqf* was for the descendants of the donor. Among the properties which were made *waqf* was a vegetable garden in the Ghawanima

quarter. The income from the *waqf* was 162 piastres a year. The donor reserved for himself the position of caretaker (not a pension, because only 6 piastres a year were allocated for this post). Each Sufi was to receive one piastre per month for food and half a piastre for accommodation (also per month).

By contrast, the 1633 *waqfiyya* by Muhammad Pasha, the governor of Jerusalem, in favour of the Zawiya al-Qadiriyya, is an entirely cash operation: 1000 silver *ghirsh as'adi*. The administrator of the *waqf* was enjoined to deal with this sum legally, producing 12 *ghirsh* for each 10 *ghirsh*, and he was to avoid *riba*. Yet the rate of interest here is extortionate. The annual income was to be 200 *ghirsh as'adi*. The principal calls on this sum were the 11 Sufis resident in the *zawiya* (6 *ghirsh* annually each, i.e. 66 in all) and the food cooked for them every Friday night (72 *ghirsh*). How they ate the rest of the time remains unclear. The provisions of the *waqf* ensured that the 11 Sufis stayed put, not being allowed to travel or to transfer their rights to another; and it was also mandatory for them to gather after every prayer and recite the Qur'an, for the benefit *inter alia* of the donor and his family. Thus the stipulations of the *waqf* translated into strictly enforced rules for the daily life of the beneficiaries.

Other arrangements in kind sometimes supplemented the standard *waqf*. Thus in the case of the Hammam al-'Ain, water from the Haram al-Sharif was exchanged for half the rent generated by the *hammam.* Sometimes, too, the supervisor of a *waqf* would lease the property in question to another person, perhaps in part at least to his own personal advantage. The massive fluctuations in the rent charged for properties—for example baths—left ample room for speculators to manipulate these prices. Such fluctuations are recorded for all kinds of foodstuffs as for other commodities, and flesh out a picture of an economy in a state of constant change.

6.5 The emphasis on minor buildings

As to the kind of buildings that were put up, they are for the most part small and insignificant, as if the intention were that they should blend into their surroundings and make no splash. In any case, the shortage of space meant that architects had to build upwards and not sideways, and not only had to take account of existing buildings but also to incorporate parts of them in the new structures which they were building. This is especially true of the area around the Ribat and Dar of Bairam Jawish, which was a prime site for Ottoman building projects. Sometimes only a small detail, like a carved decorative band on that building, which betrays the remains of the original cornice, gives clues as to how the original structure looked. But small as most of these Ottoman buildings are, they are still a *prise de possession*: like the much more splendid Mamluk buildings, they assert the presence of an external authority. The difference is that the nature of these buildings suggests that the Ottomans saw themselves as guardians and even caretakers rather than as conquerors. For much the same reason, they did not lay claim to the local Mamluk buildings. If one excludes the Khassaki Sultan, the walls and the foundations providing Jerusalem with water, the great majority of these Ottoman structures do not serve a public or welfare purpose; again, competition with the Mamluks was just not feasible, so a different message had to be transmitted.

The effects of the developments sketched in broad outline in Chapter 1 above can be read in the record of Jerusalem's Ottoman architecture. It is this that explains the multitude of minor foundations, often anonymous. These were not built to perpetuate the memory of some *amir* and perhaps provide an income for his descendants. Instead they reflect the personal piety, the desire to procure religious benefit for the Muslim community at large—and, incidentally, the straitened financial circumstances of their donors. The numerous cells and open-plan aedicules commemorating some holy event or traditional Islamic saint were too small to cost much. They were erected piecemeal, as the series of *khalwa*s on the Haram esplanade shows, at the private instigation of modest patrons, for example members of the imperial militia and often local notables such as *qadi*s or scholars. Occasionally a bolder or richer patron might, so to speak, think more laterally; thus the North-eastern Khalwa of Ahmad Pasha is the perfect match for his North-western Khalwa (colour pls. xix and xxix): the patron had secured for himself two prize locations abutting either side of the north-eastern *mawazin* colonnade. In other words, the two foundations were conceived together, to balance each other. This is, however, an exception to the general trend of piecemeal, small-scale patronage. Larger building campaigns of the kind financed from the imperial purse would have resulted in a less haphazard distribution of these buildings. The constant re-use of earlier material points in the same direction. And this in turn follows from the piecemeal nature of Ottoman patronage. True, an individual structure can display workmanship of an impeccable quality, but such excellence reflects the personal skill of that particular craftsman. It is not the natural product of sustained investment in new building. The results of that kind of investment can be seen in Mamluk Jerusalem: it raises the overall standard, from techniques of stereotomy to varieties of vaulting, from the design of an entire façade to the execution of a capital. It can be seen in the capacity to exploit a gap site or to incorporate standing elements into a new design without strain. As the building boom which had given Mamluk Jerusalem its distinctive character petered out, so did the level of expertise decline. Eventually, people must have left the construction industry for lack of work. Not surprisingly, therefore, the best of Ottoman architecture in Jerusalem is to be seen in the two generations following the Ottoman conquest, a period roughly co-terminous with the reign of Sulaiman the Magnificent, when the accumulated expertise assembled in the course of the Mamluk period could still be drawn upon and had yet to be dissipated. Typically, too, the best Ottoman work can be found in projects which involve a single master rather than an entire team. The *sabil*s are a case in point. Certainly they offer challenges of design and execution. But those challenges are well within the capacity of a single master. And the skills they require are those of the mason and the sculptor, not those of the architect.

With the single exception, as always, of the Khassaki Sultan complex (and perhaps that of Bairam Jawish as well), the buildings of Ottoman Jerusalem are deficient in the very lifeblood of architecture: a sense of space. This is a cruel irony when it is remembered that imperial Ottoman architects in the 16th century experimented more audaciously with spatial values than their counterparts in perhaps any earlier school of Islamic architecture. That was at least in part the result of massive investment in building campaigns, though of course it had much to do with the kind of building favoured by the sultans. Scarcely a distant echo of the hum of activity and eager experimentation in Istanbul can be heard in Ottoman Jerusalem. Its minarets attain barely a third of the height of those in the capital. Its monuments do not reflect the direct involvement of the top architects of Istanbul. The spatial experiment, the glamorous decoration, the precise stereotomy, the cascading curvilinear volumes of the great imperial Ottoman mosques evoked no

47 Detail of *muqarnas* cornice on Mihrab al-Sanubar (Photo Joe Rock)

comparable response in Jerusalem. And the provincial nature of this architecture became steadily more marked with the passing of time, and was compounded by the gradual decline in building activity. In the course of the 18th century, for example, not a single monument of significance was erected in Jerusalem. It is perhaps no coincidence that it is from this fallow period that some of the *musalla*s on the Haram—mere platforms of dressed stone, sometimes furnished with a *mihrab*—date. Sometimes, as in the case of the Mihrab al-Sanaubar, with its carved tulips in vases echoing a fashion which was all the rage in distant Istanbul, they stand out by virtue of some felicitous decorative detail. But for the most part they are severely plain. They attest the continuity of patronage over the Ottoman centuries and their simple form made them cheap and easy foundations. Moreover, like all the Ottoman buildings on the Haram, they respect the integrity of that sacred space, so much so that they are easily overlooked by the casual visitor. But they too, for all their modesty, have their role in daily worship.

6.6 Patrons

Who were the major patrons, and what manner of people were they? They include, apart from Bairam Jawish, who has already been discussed, Bairam Pasha, who donated 1,000 gold coins (*ghirsh*) while governor of Egypt to the buildings on the Haram; it was spent on porticoes for the Aqsa Mosque and near Bab al-Nazir and on Sabil Sha'lan. He gave a further 1,000 silver coins (*qit'a misriyya*) to the tomb of al-Nabi Da'ud, plus textiles for it. His other major donations were for 32 Qur'an readers on the Dome of the Rock platform, and for the muezzin of the Haram. A later *waqf* of his indicates that he sent ready money yearly for his *khalwa*.

The other major patrons were Ahmad Pasha, Khudawirdi Abu Saifin and Muhammad Pasha. Several of them, as well as other lesser patrons, held appointments as Ottoman governors, and it may be that patronage of local building campaigns was a case of *noblesse oblige* for such men. Sulaiman Pasha, who built the Iwan al-Sultan Mahmud II, an open-plan pavilion of Turkish type (colour pl. xxii), in 1233/1817-8 and also restored the Maqam al-Nabi Da'ud for Sultan Mahmud II in the same year, was Governor of Sidon and Tripoli. Ahmad Pasha, who built the North-western Khalwa, was Governor of Gaza; Yusuf Pasha, the patron of the *sabil*, *mihrab*, and *mastaba* which all bear the name Sha'lan, was Governor of Jerusalem; al-Hajj Arslan Pasha, who restored the Shurta al-Gharbiyya, was Governor of Jerusalem, Nablus and Gaza; Muhammad Beg, who ordered the *mihrab* niche in the Qubbat wa Mihrab al-Nabi (colour pl. xxiv), was Governor of Gaza and Jerusalem; Mustafa Agha Baraunazadeh, who ordered the domed tomb of one of the Naqshbandiyya *shaikh*s, Muhammad al-Salih al-Uzbeki, in the *zawiya* of that order, was governor of Jerusalem, as was Mustafa Agha, whose *sabil* in the Haram is the undisputed masterpiece of local 18th-century architecture (colour pls. xxvii and xxviii). Muhammad Pasha, another Governor of Jerusalem, endowed land for the Khanqah al-Maulawiyya and a plot of land on the Mount of Olives for the Sufis who came to Shaikh Muhammad al-'Alami, and the Zawiya al-As'adiyya on the same hill, in 1623. Indeed, all his

patronage was for Sufi orders and in this he is unique among the great patrons of Ottoman Jerusalem. The reasons for this remain to be discovered, but may have something to do with the way that Sufis had risen to prominence in Jerusalem in the later 17th century, a time when the city had become a specially favoured place of pilgrimage. Evliya Çelebi's report that at this time there were 'zawiyes for 70 Sufi orders' puts this kind of patronage into context. The new foundations of the late 16th and early 17th centuries which still survive in Jerusalem—Zawiya al-Maulawiyya, Zawiya al-Naqshbandiyya and Zawiya al-Qadiriyya—offer further evidence on this score, and underline the key role of Sufism rather than the orthodox religious life symbolised by the mosque, in the spirituality of the time. Among the other great patrons of Ottoman Jerusalem, Ahmad Pasha favoured the *'ulama'* and Bairam Jawish the needy.

In the later Ottoman period, four families of notables—the Husainis, 'Alamis, Nashashibis and Khalidis—figured prominently in official positions. They were later joined by the Dajanis. This concentration of influence in a few élite traditional families was a common phenomenon at the time, and can be paralleled locally, for example at Hebron and Ramla, as well as further afield in the Ottoman domains from Yemen to Morocco. But the much reduced rate of building activity in public architecture in Jerusalem, in comparison with the 16th and even the 17th century, meant that their patronage was insignificant in scale. But by virtue of the numerous *waqf*s which they controlled—many of them private and family *waqf*s—and from which they benefited in terms of salaries, posts and accommodation as well as prestige, they acquired much power and influence locally. The provisions of the *waqf* system, moreover, ensured that these benefits were available to the descendants of the original testator without the need for them to own the property itself.

7 THE PRACTICE OF ARCHITECTURE IN OTTOMAN JERUSALEM

7.1 The building trade: money, people and the law

How were these buildings financed? What workmen were needed? What controls were in place to ensure that new buildings, or for that matter repairs to existing ones, contravened neither legal regulations nor custom? Such questions are easier to ask than to answer, but the issues which they raise are central to an understanding of this architecture and how it reflected the society which produced it.

For large areas of the pre-modern Islamic world, no documents have survived which shed light on how buildings were financed. Ottoman Jerusalem is one of the relatively rare exceptions. The wealth of information in the *sijills* covers the whole range of financial issues associated with architecture—the price of land for building; the manifold expenses of construction, from materials to salaries; running costs, including staff wages; and the outgoings on repairs in subsequent centuries. While one-off cash sums might come from Istanbul or from the governors of the major cities of Egypt and the Levant, from the poll-tax levied on non-Muslims or from tax revenue collected locally, such sums were usually reserved, as already mentioned above, for high-profile projects such as the walls, the water supply or work on the Dome of the Rock and the Aqsa Mosque. But for the vast majority of buildings in Ottoman Jerusalem the principal source of financial support from start to finish was a *waqf*, very often established at the behest of a private citizen (see Chapter 6.4 above). Its value was liable to fluctuate wildly. If it was a cash deposit, the rate of interest on the capital sum could vary quite dramatically even over relatively short periods of time. If, as was more common, the *waqf* comprised the rents from industrial, domestic or agricultural property, the income depended on the regular maintenance of that property. In the course of the centuries, and often much sooner, these assets declined in value, were taken over by legal or illegal means, or disappeared altogether, taking with them the income on which the continued functioning of the foundation depended. Thus the financing of a structure was anything but a once and for all cash outlay. Rather was the typical *waqf* likely to cover the ongoing, regular expenses of a building, notably the salaries of its staff, donations in cash and kind to those whom the foundation was intended to serve—as in the case of the Sufi *zawiyas*—and the costs of maintenance and repair. A few buildings, such as Qubbat al-Nabi, Qubbat al-Arwah and Qubbat al-Khadr, were subsumed into the *waqf* of the Haram itself, which was the largest in all of Palestine.

Atallah and Natsheh have used the evidence of the *sijills* to investigate the activities of a wide range of ancillary skilled craftsmen, from the makers of brick and of pavements, to lead-pourers and those who mixed mud and *qusurmil* (wood-ash). The unskilled worker (*al-fuʿul*) naturally predominated, though even here the men were not all navvies but were subdivided according to their tasks, such as the man who sieved the soil (*al-karabili*), the man who mixed the mortar (*al-jabbal*) or who carried it (*al-tayyan*), the man who plugged small gaps in the stone coursing with small rough stones (*al-jabbash*), and the shoveller or worker with the hoe (*al-mujarifi*). Supplementary specialists included the expert in water installations (*al-qanawati*), the

48 Qubbat al-Arwah

49 Qubbat al-Khadr

porter *(al-'attal)*, the blacksmith *(al-haddad)*, the stone-cutter *(al-hajjar)*, the stone-dresser *(al-nahhat)*, the carpenter *(al-najjar)*, the man who put up the scaffolding *(al-saqqal)*, the painter and decorator *(al-naqqash)*, the water-carrier *(al-saqqa')* and the man who paved the floor *(al-muballat)*. The relative status of these and other types of workman can be deduced to some extent from the wages that they were paid (see Chapter 7.3 below).

The legal dimensions of the building tradition were multifarious. There was no shortage of red tape, as is documented by the details meticulously recorded in the registers of the Shari'a Court concerning the processes of construction, repair and destruction, all of which usually required official permission; formal complaints to the *qadi* and disputes of all kinds, from land use and land rights to questions of safety (such as ruinous walls or water contamination), privacy and public or personal inconvenience; the ratification of expenditure on *waqf* properties, as

the law required; and the frequent inspections by *ad hoc* committees often comprising at least the *qadi* or his clerk and the *mi'marbashi*. This system of checks and balances discouraged sharp practice, but by no means eradicated it, as the volume and diversity of complaints recorded in the *sijills* testify. Close control was also kept over the building activities of non-Muslims, who were required to obtain the permission of the *qadi* before undertaking projects of construction or repair.

7.2 The architects

What can be said about these architects? Salameh

has shown that Sijill 1a alone, which covers a period of fifteen months in 935-6/1529-30, mentions no less than 13 builders *(mi'mar)* active in Jerusalem at this time, eight of them from Aleppo, while the rest were, respectively, a Christian, a man from Hebron, another from Ramla and two men who bore the title of Chief Architect, Ibrahim ibn Ma'tuq al-Halabi (presumably yet another Aleppan) and Husain ibn Nammar. Such a large number of architects in what was still rather a small provincial city suggests that major building campaigns, not to mention renovations and inspections, were already under way at this time, and that they had necessitated the large-scale importation of skilled master builders from outside Jerusalem. The extent of the building campaigns under way in Jerusalem between 1529 and 1542 may be gauged by the fact that the *sijills* record the names of 46 builders. Some had no doubt been drafted in for the construction of the walls, but it is no less likely that others had flocked to Jerusalem in search of work during a relatively short-lived building boom. Yet the salient fact is that this boom seems to have owed nothing of substance to the direct contribution of architects or craftsmen from Istanbul itself, and there is no need to believe Evliya Çelebi's assertion that all the masters from Cairo, Aleppo and Damascus were sent to Jerusalem for these building campaigns.

In later years, when the building trade had regained a certain equilibrium, the master builders were mainly local men, though their towns of origin also included Hama, Antioch, Aleppo, Cairo and Istanbul as well as such Palestinian towns as Ascalon, Tripoli, Nablus, Tyre, Hebron and Ramla. Moreover, very large numbers of architects and builders are recorded in the *sijills*—128 in the 16th and 17th centuries alone, as Atallah, who has made a special study of this profession in Ottoman Jerusalem, has shown. Of these, 105 were Muslims, 22 Christians and one a Jew. Among the major discoveries made in the *sijill* records was the existence of nothing less than a dynasty of local architects whose activity spanned five generations

and almost two centuries: the Ibn Nammar family, first recorded in Sijill 1a (935-6/1529-30). Thirteen of the 17 holders of the prestigious post of *mi'marbashi* in the 16th and 17th centuries belonged to it. Their status was underlined by the use of titles implying high professional standing, such as *mu'allim*, *ustadh* or *usta*, and by other titles distinguishing them from the ruck of their peers, such as 'Chief Builder of Jerusalem the Noble *(mi'marbashi al-quds al-sharif* or *ra'is al-mi'mariyya bi'l-quds al-sharif)*. Other honorific titles contain the elements *'ain* (source) and *fakhr* (pride), and one may perhaps assume that the standing of these men found expression in the particular buildings with which they were most concerned. Paradoxically, however, it remains an open question whether they actually designed the buildings on which they worked, or whether this was a task for a *muhandis* ('engineer' or 'geometrician'). If so, no named expert of this kind is recorded in Ottoman Jerusalem, though a *qadi* is named as Sa'd al-Din ibn al-Muhandis (see p. 51 above). Several of the Ibn Nammar family played a major role in local financial and administrative affairs; they seem to have figured prominently not only as architects and builders but also as contractors and as surveyors of *waqf* properties; they also discharged accounting and legal responsibilities. Indeed, the English word 'architect' is misleading in this context, for it does not convey the range of activities carried out by the local *mi'mar* at this time. Nor does it reflect the situation which obtained in Ottoman Jerusalem, whereby a builder might at one end of the scale advise the authorities on the valuation of an estate or on where key boundaries lay and at the other end of the scale might find himself charged with demolishing a structure and carting away the rubbish thus generated. In the midst of such contrasting tasks he might be engaged in buying or selling materials or property, identifying weaknesses or danger spots in standing structures or subcontracting aspects of the building programme at a lower price and pocketing the difference.

It is worth looking a little more closely at the post of *mi'marbashi*. These men were appointed by the *qadi*, and occasionally by the direct decree of the sultan in Istanbul, for example to carry out work on the city walls. Since matters to do with construction, and indeed with building work generally, came under the jurisdiction of the *qadi*, and the law required his approval before work could begin, the professional relationship between the two was close. The remit of the *mi'marbashi* was wide, covering as it did all aspects of the construction, destruction and repair of buildings and public works, from mosques to drains, and to bring their expertise to bear in disputes between other architects and their employers, to advise on pricing policy and to ensure that once a price was set it was observed, or to deal with questions raised by members of the public in connection with architecture. This could involve adjudicating on the division of property or of common ground, making rulings on complaints, or overseeing the system of tenders, guarantees and estimates of the time needed for completion of a project. In many of these duties they seem to have discharged the functions of a modern planning department. Such a man could perhaps be described as the ombudsman of the building trade.

As noted above, it was standard practice for the *mi'marbashi* to work in close concert with the *qadi* in the inspection of buildings, canals and roads, often in the presence of witnesses or as members of an *ad hoc* committee set up by the *qadi*, submitting a report and then carrying out the repairs that the *qadi* decreed. The documents suggest, incidentally, that it was not rare for a *qadi* to possess significant expertise in matters concerning the construction and repair of all sorts of buildings, and the materials required. The responsibilities of the *mi'marbashi* also extended to auditing accounts, producing estimates and assessing rents. Altogether, then, the Chief Architect had to be a man of many talents. An efficient system of checks and balances was in operation, and—to judge by the numerous cases heard before the court—it seems to have safeguarded the interests of the ordinary citizens, whatever their confessional loyalty, with conspicuous success. Thus in the 16th and 17th centuries alone no less than 62 inspections and permits for reconstruction were recorded for Christian buildings. The picture that emerges is one of fruitful and harmonious teamwork between the law and the building trade. Nor did this prevent the *mi'marbashi* from pursuing his private business interests, provided that he held a licence to that effect from the *qadi*. Yet against this picture of the high status enjoyed by the Chief Architect—whom Atallah places on a par with the senior notables of the city—must be set the remarkable fact that the Ibn Nammar family does not appear in the epigraphic record provided by the buildings themselves, though patrons galore are mentioned in these inscriptions. This may reflect local custom, though such a custom would be atypical of the rest of the Islamic world. At all events, were it not for the Shari'a records, nothing would be known about the Ibn Nammar family—and that presumably goes for many another family of architects in other parts of the Islamic world.

Below the *mi'marbashi* were ranged architects—sometimes known as *mu'allim* or *ustadh* (both words denoting 'master') or *banna'* ('builder')—who specialised in such varied tasks as working in cemeteries; making, clearing and renovating canals; restoring lead roofs; and building the city walls.

What of salaries? Architects might be paid in money or in kind (for example wheat, olive oil and molasses), and in advance, in instalments or on completion of the project. The payment might incorporate practically all the associated costs; thus the architects charged with the rebuilding of the Bab al-Asbat minaret in 1007/1598 were to receive 200 gold *sultani*s for the work, but that sum was to include all materials (except lead) and the salaries of the work-force. Salameh has shown that the standard salary of a master builder was between 25 and 30 silver *'uthmani*s per day, which was marginally higher than the daily wage of a carpenter, a pounder *(daqqaq)* of *qusurmil*—whose particular skill lay in sealing roofs—a master plasterer of *qusurmil* or a specialist in the fitting of small stones between masonry courses *(mu'allim sirara* or *jabbash).*

7.3 Craftsmen and unskilled labourers

The previous paragraph indicates that the gap between 'architects' and certain types of 'craftsman', at least so far as their wages—if not their status— was concerned, was slight. This is best resolved by means of a comparison. The daily wages of architects (see Chapter 7.2 above) may be set against those of an artisan *(sani'*; 12.5 *'uthmanis),* workers with the hoe and rubble *(jabbal/jabish;* 10 *'uthmanis),* water-carrier (7-12 *'uthmanis),* sieveman *(gharapi'li*

or *karabili;* 8-10 *'uthmanis)* and unskilled workman *(fa'il;* 5-8 *'uthmanis);* curiously enough, a plasterer *(saqqal)* earned even less than an unskilled worker (between 1 and 5 *'uthmanis).* These figures give a rough pecking order of the workforce engaged in the building trade, but of course they reveal little about the level of remuneration which the most distinguished members of the profession could command.

Research by Natsheh has established that the tools and related objects used by local craftsmen included shovels, ropes, axes, baskets, scales, clamps and pulley blocks. But much remains to be done, especially in identifying the various types of chisel used in the dressing of stone; the very varied surfaces of the stonework in these Ottoman buildings indicate that a correspondingly wide range of tools was used, and their identification might help—as in other periods of architectural history—in solving problems of dating or in determining the provenance of craftsmen.

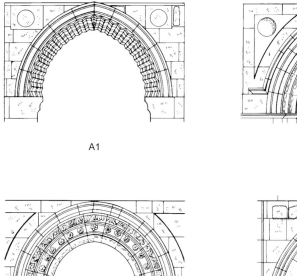

A1

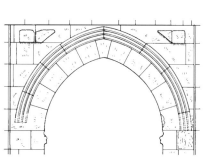

A2

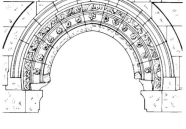

A3

A4

50 Arches

8   BUILDING TYPES

8.1 Public architecture

The survival of almost sixty public structures of Ottoman date in Jerusalem, many of them accurately dated or datable by endowments preserved in the *sijill*s, makes it possible to assess the local style in the round (see Chapter 5.5 above). Happily, too, these buildings are of the most varied type: open-plan aedicules commemorating some venerated prophet; simple local mosques; *zawiya*s serving the Sufis living in or visiting the city, sometimes so placed that buildings for separate *tariqa*s adjoin each other; tiny non-residential open-air *madrasa*s, which also served to house the *shaikh* in charge; *sabil*s; *mastaba*s; minarets; simple domed cells; and two extensive charitable foundations fulfilling a wide range of functions.

Only a few of these building types are numerous enough to justify a general discussion. The *sabil*s are an obvious case; they number 13, though when Evliya Çelebi visited Jerusalem in 1082/1672 there were 61. Their form varies, from largely two-dimensional framed arches with a trough (sometimes a re-used antique or Christian sarcophagus) beneath them to free-standing domed squares. Both types are found from early Ottoman times in Jerusalem and both have Turkish elements. Indeed, the earliest of them—the free-standing Sabil of Qasim Pasha (933/1527)—is a canopied octagonal *shadirvan* of distinctively Turkish type. The first kind, which is essentially two-dimensional, owes something to the visual vocabulary of the Mamluk portal, which in some cases can be linked with the portals of Saljuq Anatolia. Related *sabil*s are known in Mamluk Aleppo, in Maghribi architecture as far west as Fez and, above all, in

Istanbul, where—according to Aslanapa—there were once 800 such structures. This makes Istanbul the most obvious source of inspiration, but clearly the type was widespread throughout the western Islamic world. The architectural vocabulary of the two-dimensional *sabil*s features engaged columns comprising a cluster of partially braided colonnettes, chevron or gadrooned arch profiles, the lavish use of Crusader *spolia* and pronounced volutes ending in a small circle.

Documentary evidence shows that a large group of them, dating from the later 1530s, were intended as a package: Sabil Bab al-Nazir (colour pl. xxxi), which was made *waqf* in the name of Sultan Sulaiman five years after it was constructed, was one of nine *sabil*s—which indicates that some of them have vanished in the course of the centuries. What was their purpose? At the most obvious level they have to do with the provision of water for the public, and are thus a work of charity which is recommended in the Qur'an. Some refer in their inscriptions to the hope of the water of Paradise and compare their water to the water of Paradise. But other factors must also be considered. Several *sabil*s are dated to the month of Muharram, and the semantic connection of that word with sanctity, and hence purity, is entirely appropriate to their function of aiding ritual purity. Not to be overlooked, either, are the Shi'ite pilgrims who thronged to the city; for them, there would be the added associations of the awful thirst suffered by the martyrs of Karbala. Indeed, the now vanished Sabil al-Husaini of 1724-5 refers in its surviving inscription to al-Husain the son of 'Ali b. Abi Talib, and thus to the battle of Karbala. The implication is that all who drank from the *sabil*

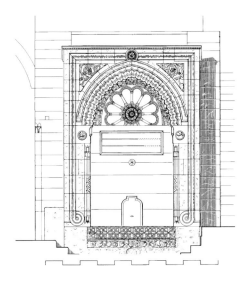

51 Sabil Bab al-Silsila, elevation

52 Sabil al-Wad, elevation

were expected to pray for al-Husain. The family name of the founder, as it happens, was al-Husaini. It may also be relevant to some of these *sabil*s that—as the local people would have known—the 16th Muharram was the day that Jerusalem was selected as the *qibla*. Both Sabil Sha'lan and Sabil Bab al-'Atm have prayer facilities attached (in the former case both a *mihrab* and a *mastaba*); perhaps it was usual to pray after drinking, but in any case the *sabil* in these two cases seems to have been intended for ablution as well as drinking. The latter was surely the primary purpose of such structures; an inscription on the Sabil al-Shurbaji of 1097/1685-6 proclaims "Abd al-Karim al-Shurbaji built the *sabil* so that thirsty people might drink'. Hence, too, their location at traffic nodes so that they could serve the largest number of people—thus Bab al-'Atm and Sabil Qasim Pasha are both placed near major gates giving access to the Haram. The fact that these *sabil*s are of such different sizes and designs suggests that they were the work of various craftsmen, and that there was little overall supervision. Certainly the contrast between the most elaborate (Sabil Bab al-Silsila: colour pl. xxxii) and the simplest of all (Sabil Bab Sitti Maryam) points in that direction. Not all of the surviving

*sabil*s were the work of Sultan Sulaiman, as shown by the *sabil*s from later Ottoman times, which favour the form of a free-standing square with a low dome and one, two or three windows. Sabil Bab al-Maghariba, for example, may be one of three built, according to Evliya Çelebi, by Danyal Pasha. Like other *sabil*s, it was endowed—in this case, with a brass cauldron and with money for buckets, ropes, and the daily hire of a water carrier who was charged with filling and cleaning the trough every day and with the lighting of an oil lamp for the hours of darkness. In some cases the *waqf* paid for a caretaker whose job it was to oversee repairs and to collect the revenue from the *waqf*.

The *sabil* has a strong claim to be the most typical building type of Ottoman Jerusalem, for it spans most of the Ottoman period, from Sulaiman's foundations to the *sabil* of Mustafa Agha some two centuries later (colour pl. xxviii). It would be hard to choose a more fitting *envoi* for the type. It is a poised and elegant building, delicately proportioned, whose high plinth is an integral part of the design. A little gem and easily the finest building of the 18th century in Jerusalem, it fits perfectly into its context—the long arcade bordering the Haram precinct.

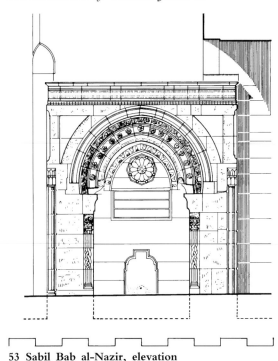

53 Sabil Bab al-Nazir, elevation

54 Sabil Sha'lan, north elevation

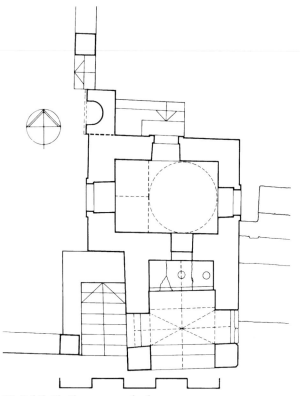

55 Sabil Sha'lan, ground plan

Still commoner are the domed squares which border the Haram or are scattered around it. Some are commemorative structures of religious intent, to which their *mihrab*s testify; sometimes they are connected with the Haram itself and sometimes with a specific prophet or celebrated individual, and many of them were a focus of pilgrimage. The Qubbat Yusuf Agha of 1681 is typical of many of these little buildings in its extremely plain domed structure and in its isolation. Although certain formal sub-divisions for such structures do suggest themselves, these buildings follow a formula deeply rooted in Ottoman architecture from the early 14th century onwards. It was a notably flexible formula: effective on both a small and a large scale, it could accommodate adjoining structures without losing its character, and it readily lent itself to repetition. These qualities are well illustrated in the Hujrat Muhammad Amir Liwa' al-Quds, a pair of adjoining domed squares which formerly had a three-domed portico, a canonical form in Ottoman Anatolia. The Khalwa al-Junbalatiyya, on the other hand, formerly had a two-bayed porch (the stone here

has weathered only a little, which suggests that the porch was removed only recently), while only a platform remains in the case of the Madrasa of Ahmad Pasha—presumably an open-air *madrasa*, with the *khalwa* acting as the accommodation for the *shaikh* in charge, and with its own water supply via an underground cistern. Indeed, the disappearance of the porticoes of these cells seems to be a general and as yet unexplained pattern. These porches, which are generally salient, attest the impact of forms developed in Ottoman Turkey. In a few cases, the porches have been rebuilt and

56 Hujrat Muhammad Amir Liwa' al-Quds, west and north façades

the bases of their columns now serve as capitals just as elsewhere capitals serve as bases, as at the North-western Khalwa of Ahmad Pasha. This cavalier attitude to re-used material, which will shortly be discussed in greater detail, is typical of the architecture of Ottoman Jerusalem.

Their purpose—principally to serve Sufis and the poor—has been outlined briefly above, but it is worth investigating the matter in a little more detail, particularly as this building type is not only very popular in Ottoman Jerusalem (15 examples are known) but also because the free-standing *khalwa*s which take this form are themselves an innovation in the city. A favoured setting for them was at the junction of the upper and lower terraces of the Haram. Some of them

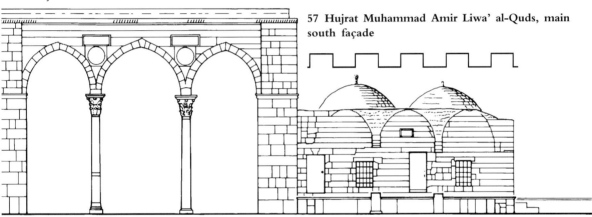

57 Hujrat Muhammad Amir Liwa' al-Quds, main south façade

58 Hujrat Muhammad Amir Liwa' al-Quds, north façade

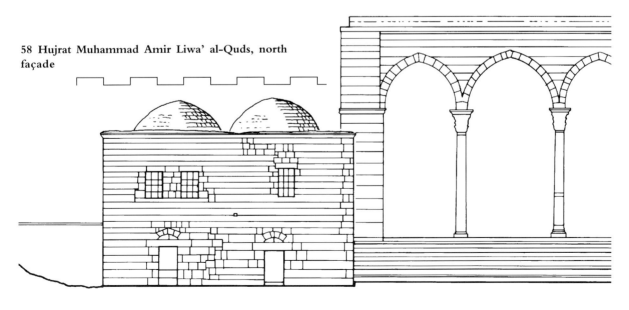

probably housed the staff of the Haram, as is still the case for many of them, such as Khalwat Qitas, or Khalwat Parwiz, which is now the office of the Guards of the Noble Sanctuary, or the Qubbat Yusuf Agha, now the ticket office to the Haram. Other *khalwa*s served for teaching and for Qur'an recitation. On the other hand, Evliya Çelebi writes of pilgrims being lent a cell for the duration of their visit—presumably pilgrims of a certain social standing. A rather different fate befell the Qubbat al-Khadr: in time it lost its original meaning, and was then used to store material belonging to the Aqsa Mosque; other *khalwa*s also served as storage space, for example to hold the shoes of visitors to the Haram. This shifting of meaning, associations and functions from one site to another is typical of the Haram, as is the use of multiple names for the same site, which also reflects such changes. The inscription of the Khalwat al-Dajani (1138/1725-6) calls it a *makan*—'place'—as if the intention were to leave its actual function as broad as possible. Perhaps al-Dajani's primary aim was to erect a building—any building—on this coveted site. Its façades are grossly irregular, suggesting that its position, tucked into a corner of the staircase to the upper terrace, was the key factor in its design. Further information is given in the *waqf* for the North-western Khalwa of Ahmad Pasha, which stipulates that he has 'constructed and endowed cells in the mosque of Jerusalem. He has appointed to each cell a group of scholars from Jerusalem and allocated expenditure . . .' He specifies the scholars, who are members of the Qadiriyya order, by name. Some of the money, as noted earlier, is for oil for the lamp—and also for restoring the doors. Although the *waqf* envisaged that only four students should study here, it nevertheless decreed that they should be taught by the best scholar of the age. This use of the *khalwa* form to discharge at least some of the functions of a *madrasa*, even if only on a lilliputian scale, is fully in accord with that the practice so common in Islamic architecture generally of using a single form for a variety of quite disparate functions. There

was no sense that a given form necessarily connoted a single purpose. Sometimes the sites chosen have their own particular felicity; thus the two *khalwa*s of Ahmad Pasha constitute a perfect match thanks to the choice of site, as already explained. Here the patron had managed to secure for himself two prize locations abutting either side of the north-east *mawazin* colonnade (colour pl. xix). Clearly these two foundations were conceived together and intended to balance one another.

Another common form was the open-plan octagonal (or occasionally hexagonal) aedicule, a type encountered all over the Muslim world at least from the tenth century onwards and functioning not only as a commemorative building—the category to which the many examples at Jerusalem belong—but also as a fountain (Ma'arrat al-Nu'man, Syria) or a mausoleum (Van, Turkey). The examples on the Haram are commemorative and the case of the two structures erected by Yusuf Agha in 1681—the Qubbat Yusuf (an open-plan aedicule: colour pl. xxiii) and the Qubbat Yusuf Agha (a closed domed square)—clearly suggest that, despite the identical terminology, different forms connoted different functions in Jerusalem at that time.

Of the 29 *mihrab*s of Ottoman date, most of them in the Haram, which are currently known, the great majority are of traditional design, namely built into a *qibla* wall and, whether of flat or concave type, comprising an arch enclosed within a rectangular frame. Yet for the most part they depart from the norm in that they are rigorously unadorned. Two other types of *mihrab* are known, each represented by three examples only: *mihrab*s of coloured marble or monochrome slabs inlaid into the floor and associated with a structure (their dating is a matter of dispute); and free-standing *mihrab*s comprising a low wall with a *mihrab* in it or inlaid in the floor. These last two types, which are rare in Islamic architecture, owe much to the role of Jerusalem as a focus for pilgrimage, for they are associated with sites of religious importance. It is quite possible that the floor *mihrab* was

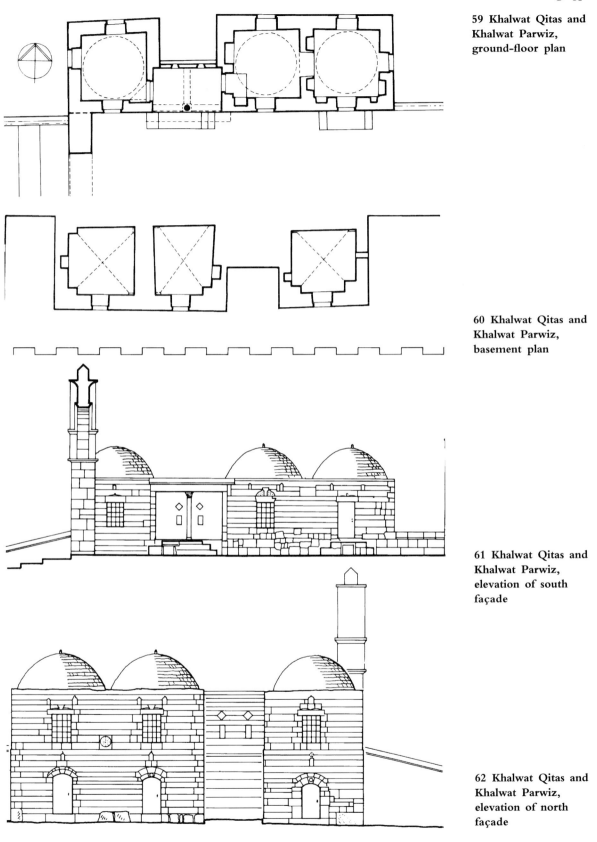

59 Khalwat Qitas and
Khalwat Parwiz,
ground-floor plan

60 Khalwat Qitas and
Khalwat Parwiz,
basement plan

61 Khalwat Qitas and
Khalwat Parwiz,
elevation of south
façade

62 Khalwat Qitas and
Khalwat Parwiz,
elevation of north
façade

deliberately developed in pre-Ottoman times as a means of facilitating prayer in an environment—the upper terrace of the Haram—where it was important to preserve an uncluttered space, and that it was only in Ottoman times that this ban on subsidiary buildings there was relaxed.

As noted earlier, no mosques of importance were built in the city in the Ottoman period. Among the minor local mosques one might single out the Masjid al-Qaimari, hard to date but of a single-unit domed type found throughout the Ottoman domains, and the mosque in the Zawiya al-Qadiriyya (1047/1643-4) which also follows a familiar Ottoman formula, whereby two domed units are divided by a transverse arch. Of the 70 Sufi orders for which *zawiya*s existed in Jerusalem at the time of Evliya Çelebi's visit in 1082/1672, four survive: al-Zawiya al-Hamra', al-Zawiya or al-Khanqah al-Maulawiyya, al-Zawiya al-Naqshbandiyya and al-Zawiya al-Qadiriyya, all of them sponsored by governors who favoured the Sufis. The standard plan featured an open courtyard surrounded by cells and furnished with a cistern and a mosque, a hall for Sufi ceremonies and a kitchen.

Even stranger, perhaps, than the relative absence of mosques is the almost total absence of mausolea in Ottoman Jerusalem, especially when one considers their popularity in the Mamluk period in Jerusalem. The principal exception is the mausoleum within the Khassaki Sultan complex, whose location, within a larger compound whose purpose is not primarily a funerary one, follows earlier local precedent. This dearth of funerary architecture (four insignificant tomb chambers in all) may have something to do with the very short tenure of the Ottoman governors of the city, which in turn found expression in the lack of major pious foundations. The *madrasa* is just as rare as the mosque and the mausoleum; indeed, it is food for thought that these three building types, the most popular in the public architecture of the Islamic world, are easily outnumbered in Ottoman Jerusalem by *sabil*s, *khalwa*s and commemorative religious

buildings: clear proof, if any were needed, that Jerusalem in this period was a law to itself.

8.2 Industrial and vernacular architecture

Nor should one forget structures of a more vernacular or industrial type, though these are not mentioned in any detail in this book. Among the public buildings, baths *(hammam*s) take pride of

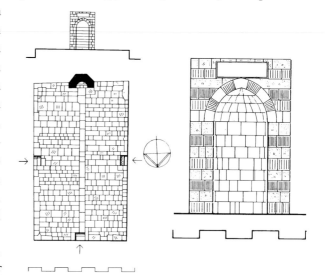

63 **Mihrab 'Ali Pasha, plan and elevation**

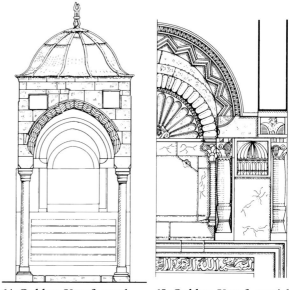

64 **Qubbat Yusuf, north elevation**

65 **Qubbat Yusuf, partial elevation, south wall**

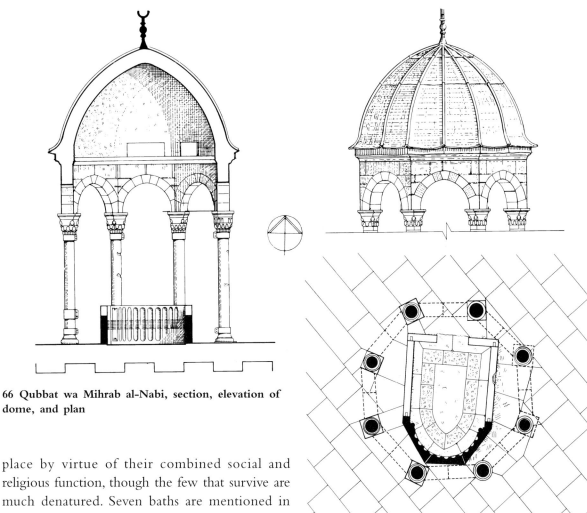

66 Qubbat wa Mihrab al-Nabi, section, elevation of dome, and plan

place by virtue of their combined social and religious function, though the few that survive are much denatured. Seven baths are mentioned in the *sijill*s, four of them in the close vicinity of the Haram al-Sharif and therefore presumably intended at least in part for ritual ablution, though their cost—one and a half *dirham*s per man and two and a half *dirham*s (with henna) for women— suggests that their frequent use was a privilege reserved for the well-to-do. They were open to all, irrespective of religious affiliation; even Western visitors used them. Their resultant value as a source of revenue made them an obvious channel for entrepreneurs, and there are frequent references in the *sijill*s to how administrators of *hammam*s (all of which were *waqf* properties)—such as the imam of the Dome of the Rock, Shaikh Abu'l-Fath ibn Fityan—rented them out at a profit. The *hammami*, or keeper of the bath, paid a fixed rent, often on an annual basis, and it was of course up to him to

make his investment pay. Other arrangements in kind sometimes supplemented the standard *waqf*. Thus in the case of the Hammam al-'Ain, water from the Haram al-Sharif was exchanged for half the rent generated by the *hammam*. In the course of the Ottoman period, the functioning public baths seem to have numbered six: al-'Ain, al-Shifa', al-Batrak, al-Sultan, al-Sayyida Maryam, and al-Jamal. Their names were, however, subject to constant change, which explains why it seems (erroneously) that more baths are mentioned in the written sources. Thus Hammam al-Jamal is referred to by Evliya Çelebi as Hammam al-Sakhra, perhaps because its endowment was from that of the Dome of the Rock. The social role of the

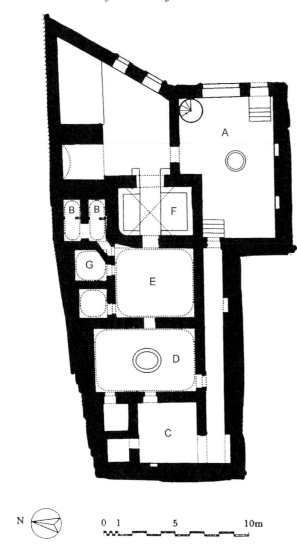

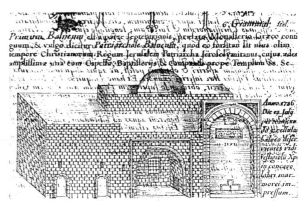

68 Horn's illustration of Hammam al-Sayyida Maryam in the 18th century (photograph Biblioteca Vaticana, Rome, MS. Lat. 9233)

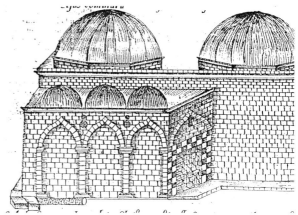

69 Horn's illustration of Hammam al-Sultan (photograph Biblioteca Vaticana, Rome, MS. Lat. 9233)

67 Plan of Hammam al-Sayyida Maryam

hammam should not be overlooked, especially in the case of women, for visits to the bath provided them with regular opportunities to meet other women outside the family circle. The fact that the *hammam* was open on a daily basis (in the 18th century, the hours for men were from 2 a.m. until midday and for women from midday until night) meant that it was an indispensable element in fostering social relationships—and it featured largely in the key rites of passage. Thus it was established practice for the bride to go to the bath the day before her marriage, and the *hammam* would be hired for the entire day for the associated celebrations and rituals.

Two *khan*s survive (one mentioned in the endowment deed of Khassaki Sultan as part of that complex, the other, Khan al-Sha'ara, in the present Jewish quarter). The *sijill*s mention several functioning *khan*s *intra muros*, namely Khan al-Wakala, Khan al-Ghadiriyya, Khan Bab al-'Amud, the Khan of the Melons, Khan al-Fakhriyya, Khan Daraj al-'Ain, Khan al-Fahm, Khan Wad al-Tawahiyya and Khan al-Quttain; some of these were *waqf*s and produced rental income. Two *ribat*s are mentioned in the *sijill*s—the richly endowed Mamluk Ribat al-Mansuri, which in 941/1534 was leased for the substantial sum of 20,000 *'uthmani*s per year, and, opposite it on the same street, the Ribat of 'Ala' al-Din al-Basir; the expenses of its seventeen residents were met from the rent of the Hammam 'Ala' al-Din. A third and extremely dilapidated *ribat* was turned into a vegetable garden in 943/1537. The same change of function overtook many *zawiya*s, almshouses for the poor, which were turned into private residences and then rented out. There were at least four prisons, but little is known about them.

The surviving industrial buildings include over a score of bakeries (here close dating is particularly difficult); stables; oil presses (though only two now survive, whereas more than a score were in operation a generation ago and for most of the Ottoman period only four or five); and soap factories. The trade in oil and soap with Egypt was particularly lively. A dozen large markets, notably Suq Khan al-Zait, Suq al-'Attarin, Suq al-Lahhamin, Suq al-Khuwajat, and Suq al-Husur, were in operation. Some of these were newly founded in the Ottoman period, others were older but still in use under their earlier names, and yet others were known by more than one name. In some cases the location and function of a market has remained stable for almost a millennium (e.g. the triple market founded by Queen Melisande in the 12th century). The number of these markets is a useful index for the city's economic activity in Ottoman times, though it is of little use in plotting the frequent and vertiginous rise and fall in the prices of given commodities. An effective guild system organised the functioning, taxation, and, where necessary, policing of these various industries. Indeed, in the late 17th century there were separate guilds for doctors and surgeons; veterinary surgeons; tanners; shoemakers; weavers; millers; tailors; public criers; glassmakers; porters of corpses; earth-carriers; water carriers; sheep-skinners; candle-makers; dyers; goldsmiths; and knife-makers and swordsmiths. The range of these guilds is a reminder that for centuries Jerusalem has functioned as the market town for its region. Of other establishments, such as granaries, tanneries, dye-works, fruit presses, mills and pottery workshops, little or no trace remains; in some of these cases the building within which the business

in question was carried out was probably had little to distinguish it from an ordinary house or shop. Evliya Çelebi, writing in the second half of the 17th century, records that the city had 2,045 shops. These probably comprised little more than adjoining rectangular spaces opening onto the street and with a raised bench in front.

It should be noted that after 1840, with the rapid increase of the population (from *c.* 9,000 in 1820 to *c.* 51,000 in 1896) and the concomitant growth of the tourist trade, the development of new export industries such as fruit and wine, the incursions of various Western powers and the rise of an Arab entrepreneurial class, the nature of economic life in Jerusalem underwent drastic change. This was manifested in a building boom which permanently changed the face of the city. The details of this boom, however, fall outside the scope of this book.

8.3 Domestic architecture

At least thirty examples of the *dar* or private house for the élite survive. Some are extremely rare, like the Dar Bairam Jawish, of 953/1546, which is the only house datable to the sixteenth century in Jerusalem (colour pl. xviii). Its north and south fronts both have an arch with a double tier of voussoirs, as does the façade of the Ribat of Bairam Jawish. The lack of comparable structures makes it difficult to assess the originality of this feature. More generally, there are no extant Mamluk precedents for this *dar*; the most appropriate parallel is the Dar of Sitt Tunshuq, which is a palace rather than the private house of a notable. Another exception is the Dar al-'Izz of 1790-1, perhaps built as a private commercial guesthouse; this is a rare example of a dated secular private building in Ottoman Jerusalem, notable for the presence of a courtyard and garden on the first floor.

Since élite Ottoman housing does not figure largely in the book, it may be useful to give here a generic description of the type. A

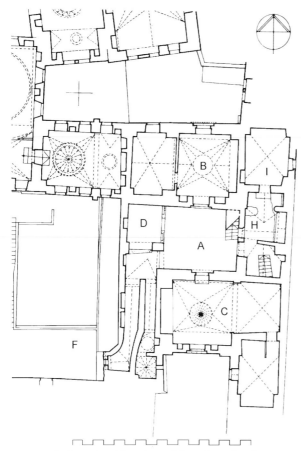

70 Dar Bairam Jawish, plan of first-floor level

71 First floor window with a timber shutter, situated above the main door of Bait Mamluk

72 Section of Bait Mamluk

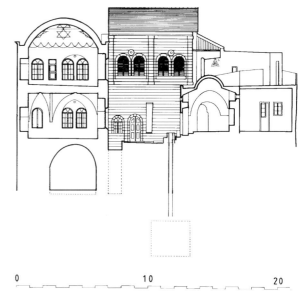

courtyard at ground floor level surrounded by utility rooms is reached by a single external entrance. The principal rooms are at first-floor level and are reached by a staircase which gives onto a balcony overlooking the courtyard. These are the rooms which contain ornament: external carved window frames, carved and painted plaster, and domes on octagons, so low that they are often only just visible from the street. In rare cases (mostly in 19th-century houses owned by the major local families: Husaini, Nusaibah, Khalidi and Nashashibi), the ceilings were painted (colour pl. xiii), with a repertoire of themes borrowed either from Istanbul or from Europe: night skies scattered with stars, *rocaille* ornament, rosettes, cartouches, still-life motifs, vases and bouquets of flowers, and—for houses built for members of the Christian élite—*putti* and saints. Carving sometimes highlighted this decoration. Some vernacular Ottoman houses are up to three storeys high, and narrow single or paired rectangular windows and suspended buttresses (that is, buttresses built into the wall but standing proud of it) enliven their outer walls. Although they are scattered all over the Muslim quarter, clusters of two or more of them are to be found in ʿAqabat al-Shaikh Rihan, Tariq Bab al-Silsila, Tariq al-Hakkari, ʿAqabat al-Khalidiyya, ʿAqabat al-Maulawiyya and especially ʿAqabat al-Saraya. Nor should one forget more humble types of dwelling, notably the *haush*. Many of these units still survive in Jerusalem; they house as many as six families apiece. They represent a remarkably economical exploitation of the very limited space for building available in the Old City, for they are fitted into the irregular spaces left over between larger structures, and are capable of expansion not only laterally but also vertically for several low storeys. Haush al-Hilu, for example, is entered by a low vaulted passage from ʿAqabat al-Saraya; this leads into the first courtyard. Off this courtyard are passages which lead to further dwellings which seem eventually to back on to Khassaki Sultan and Haush Shawish. Thus every crevice of space is utilised.

The evidence accumulated by Salameh on the basis of his researches in the *sijill*s adds much extra information about how these houses functioned in Ottoman times. A cistern for collecting rainwater was a standard feature and many houses had such elements as a stable, a storage area for straw, an open courtyard, a latrine, a kitchen, an *iwan*, an upper floor and even a third storey (which implies that there was already pressure on domestic living space in the city despite the presence of many derelict buildings). Many *haush*es in particular were derelict because people preferred to live in private houses rather than in compounds. Christians and Jews tended to remain within their own quarters.

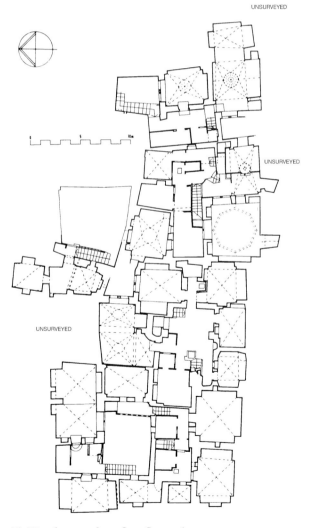

73 Haush complex, first-floor plan

9   ARCHITECTURAL STYLE IN OTTOMAN JERUSALEM: FORM, MATERIALS, TECHNIQUE AND DECORATION

9.1 The context

The picture of limited resources and limited perspectives outlined above does not tell the whole story. As Eric Schroeder has wittily said, 'To eschew the sacred wafer of Genius is no hardship to a man who chews the beefsteak of honest performance'. Good architecture is often a matter of good manners. And Jerusalem has long had a solid tradition in this respect. The ready availability of good building stone can be recognised at a glance in many an old street of the city. A city in which dressed stone is the standard building material—San'a' is another example—will never lack stone-cutters and masons and the centuries of practical experience which they bring to their trade. Hence, at minimum, the sense of comfortable rightness, and more often the sober elegance, that characterises most Ottoman public buildings in Jerusalem. This architecture is admittedly not spectacular, but it is consistently good to look at. The architects took care that however widely rubble masonry and concealing layers of plaster were used inside a building, the best-quality stonework would be saved for the exterior.

9.2 The nature of the cityscape

Nonetheless, for all this variety of public, industrial, commercial, vernacular and private buildings, there are some telling absences which are enough in themselves to define Jerusalem as an economic and architectural backwater. The lack of major Ottoman mosques, *madrasa*s, palaces, and caravansarais clinches this unflattering description.

The picture is very different from that of Aleppo and Damascus in Ottoman times, as already stated. The buildings in those cities are not only much more numerous—as is only to be expected given their much greater size—but of much higher technical quality, larger, more ambitious, and much more lavishly decorated. Thus their impact in the urban environment is much more assertive than those of Jerusalem, with their marked absence of spectacular portals, large domes, lofty minarets and elaborate external decoration.

Yet this very remoteness from the world of the great provincial cities, let alone from the imperial Ottoman metropolis itself, brings

74 Jaffa Gate area in the Old City (late 1870s) (Bonfils, Collection of Fouad Debbas, Archives for Historical Documentation)

75 Steps leading to the Holy Sepulchre (Bonfils 848, coutesy of the Fine Arts Library, Harvard College Library)

76 'Christian Street', scene from a stereograph, *c.* 1900 (Underwood and Underwood, Hummel Collection)

concomitant advantages in its train. Jerusalem offers an excellent opportunity to investigate the physical environment of a small provincial Ottoman town of only minor commercial importance. Despite the ravages of war and the relentless pressures of commercial and industrial development, despite its ballooning population and its flawed record of conserving historic buildings, the Old City, at the outset of the new millennium, can claim—against all odds—to preserve the essence of a pre-modern Palestinian town. It is wonderfully all of a piece. This is due in large measure to its wealth of domestic and vernacular architecture built in the local stone, amidst which the Ottoman public buildings are randomly scattered. In other words, it is precisely because they have not lost their original setting—the workaday context out of which they grew—that these public buildings seem so natural a part of the cityscape. They are constructed of the selfsame local stone as the streets and houses all around them. Those streets maintain a comfortable human scale; apart from the main arterial thoroughfares, they are neither so wide as

to be grand nor so narrow as to be unpleasantly constricting. Designed for pedestrians and animals only—there are no cars—they follow the natural topography in their rise and fall, with short flights of wide, easily negotiable steps to mark transitions or to modulate a long vista. Our great-grandparents would still recognise this city.

This network of narrow alleyways is the determining feature of the urban structure; it explains the absence of open spaces and hence the inward-looking nature of the whole urban environment. Even the Haram al-Sharif, whose amplitude is so at variance with the constriction of the rest of the city, is still turned in upon itself. With the obvious exception of the Dome of the Rock, which broadcasts its personality to the city at large, it does not look outwards to a wider world. This lack of interest in external façades is common enough in Islamic architecture and has as its natural corollary a focus on interior space. Thus courtyards serve as the lungs of old Jerusalem, especially given the fact that as a walled city it has been able to absorb an increasing population only by putting an equally increasing pressure on the limited space available. That is why, for example, house doors open directly onto the street, why one tier of housing is piled upon another (all can benefit from the same courtyard even though light and ventilation are progressively reduced), and why new buildings over the centuries have had to make do with gap sites. Hence the piecemeal nature of the old city when it is studied as a whole.

A brief look at one of the favourite devices for creating more space, apparently out of nowhere, will put these remarks into perspective. At second-storey level or above, arches like flying buttresses bridge the street (hence their name: *qantara*) and support passageways and rooms, thus making it possible for a single house to spread comfortably across a public thoroughfare. It is also common for the bridge to belong exclusively to the house on one side of the street, so that the wall of the house opposite serves only as a support for one end of the bridge. Yet such bridges, which seem to float above the street, and do indeed belong to another and private world, also serve a structural purpose, a role taken up by the sequences of round-headed and flat-topped arches which create sudden vistas down a narrow alley. Over two dozen *qanatir* survive, enough to make them a distinctive hallmark of local architecture. Often they are to be found in areas where space for building was particularly short, and thus coveted. It is worth reflecting that the extra domestic space won by these bridges, and by the oriel windows which are an equally common feature of the cityscape, and which allow the occupants of a house a better view of the street below, is at the expense of an encroachment on public space, which is already severely limited. It should be noted, too, that the greater height above ground level of the rooms carried by these *qanatir* could give a splendid view which made up for their sometimes considerable distance from the Haram, the natural focus of the Muslim city.

This, then, is a cityscape still not disfigured by modern boulevards and as a result not only the private housing but also the commercial life of the Old City, with its traditional pattern of small shops clustered together according to their specialties, has not yet given way to quantities of supermarkets, large retail outlets, just as traditional housing has not yet lost ground to apartment blocks and high-rise hotels. The briefest glance at Aleppo and Damascus, cities which have lost much of their pre-19th century fabric, shows how precious this heritage of Jerusalem is. What has been conserved, moreover, is not only the pre-modern fabric of the town but also much of the traditional way of life that goes with it. All this makes Jerusalem—quite aside from its worldwide religious and political importance—exceptional among the cities of the Middle East. Even in the 19th century this special quality was recognised by foreign visitors who had seen other cities in the region. Thus Mark Twain wrote in 1869 that Jerusalem 'is knobbly with countless little domes as a prison door with boltheads. Every house has from one to half a dozen of these white plastered domes of stone, broad and low, sitting in the centre of, or in a cluster, upon the flat roof … (it is) the knobbliest city in the world, except Constantinople.' Only rarely were these domes graced with drums to lend them greater height. Thus the overall aspect of the city when viewed from a distance or a height was of a concourse of molehills, with a correspondingly sculptural quality. It is worth remembering, too, that in more prosperous times the old city had a distinctively different aspect from that which it now presents, for the houses were formerly whitewashed and plastered smooth. This outer coat provided protection against heavy rain and even snow—for Jerusalem is no stranger to severe winter weather—but had the no less important aesthetic role of lightening the buildings which it covered. In a climate where strong sunlight is the norm, the effect was to heighten the overall tonal impact of such buildings clustered together, and indeed to make them dazzling. The uneven rate at which this outer plastering was applied and renewed meant that there was never any lack of tonal contrast between brand-new and age-stained plaster, or indeed surfaces where the plaster rendering had disappeared. Altogether, then, thanks to both direct and reflected light, the city would have been much brighter and whiter in the Ottoman centuries than it is now. Extra protection from the weather came from stone tiles and lead roofs, and the colours of

77 Al-'Imara al-'Amira (Khassaki Sultan), view over kitchen roof to Dome of the Rock

these materials would have added a richer texture to the city. These effects are now largely things of the past, and they show that without constant upkeep this heritage is vulnerable. Deliberate destruction has also taken its toll: the fate of the Maghariba quarter, rapidly razed after the 1967 war and languishing in a planners' limbo ever since, is a stark reminder of how quickly and irretrievably this cityscape can be destroyed.

9.3 Building materials

Invaluable work has been done by Atallah on building materials. His work on the *sijills* reveals the various types of stone in common use: rubble; fire-blackened rubble and a wide range of stones whose exact significance is hard to determine

78 Haram al-Sharif (1858), with the Maghribi Quarter, demolished in 1967 (M J Diness, John Barnier Collection, Archives for Historical Documentation)

(al-ayyubi, al-'aqadi, al-mazzi, al-manhut, al-salb, al-qantari and *al-mamillawi)* but which in their variety alone give some idea of how specialised this industry was. Yet another category was paving stones *(balat)*, of which at least five separate varieties, independent of distinctions of colour, are recorded. Orders for stones were usually in multiples of a hundred and could rise to 3,000. It was common practice to specify the exact size of the stones required, and these dimensions were given in terms of fingers and of fractions of an arm. Certain types of stone, such as paving or framing slabs, required a lengthy process of preparation which culminated in polishing them with sand. The people of Dair Yasin specialised in the production of such slabs, a further clue to the degree of specialisation that reigned in this industry.

In a city where dressed stone was the standard building material, even debris had its value; in 937/1530-1, five hundred stones from the ruinous Dar Ibn al-Sa'r were sold for a silver *halabi* apiece, and ruined buildings were sought after not only because of the value of their land but also for the re-sale value of their stones. Ancient structures from Crusader and even Roman times were also robbed for stones. Marble, too, was avidly collected from ruined buildings, though its scarcity meant that it was reserved for key areas such as lintels, *mihrabs* and capitals. Some of the *qusur* or palatial summer-houses outside the Old City could yield as many as 3,000 stones. The use of recycled material continued throughout most of the Ottoman period, from the stones of Qa'it Bay's Ashrafiyya *madrasa* re-used in the Khassaki Sultan in the mid-16th century to the Iwan al-Sultan Mahmud II in the 19th century. All this points to a chronic shortage of high-grade dressed stone, a fact perhaps to be explained by the lack of local quarries. No reference to such quarries has been found in the *sijill*s, which is a telling omission in view of the wealth of detail which they provide on all aspects of the building trade.

Apart from stone, two materials were of crucial importance in construction work: mortar

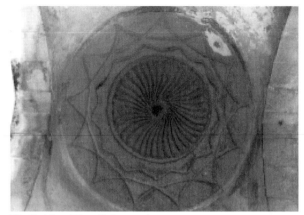

79 Qubbat Yusuf, inner dome

80 Qubbat Yusuf, general side view

81 Qubbat Yusuf, general view from front

82 Qubbat Yusuf, west side panel detail

(shid) and *qusurmil*. Mortar, whose price could vary from 10 to 72 *halabi*s per donkey-load, depending at least in part on transportation costs, was for the most part produced in the villages around

Jerusalem. The quality of its lime (manufactured in the same 11 villages) was subject to official inspection and its price could fluctuate severely—in one document in Sijill 8:144 the cost of a *qintar* of lime varies from 12 to 60 *'uthmani*s. The cost of transportation more than doubled its price. *Qusurmil* may be defined as the ashy residue left after the burning of wood for heating the water used in the numerous *hammam*s of the city. It served, in combination with other substances, for flooring and as a form of harling to seal a wall or roof surface, and had to be sifted and kneaded before it could be used. Its price varied from 4 to 10 *halabi*s per donkey-load. Sand was cheaper than either mortar or *qusurmil* but was less frequently used, and even rarer materials included baked brick *(tub mashwi)*, heat-resistant irregular stone blocks *(jabbsh nari)*, red earth *(turab ahmar)*, chalk *(huwar)* and brick dust *(humra)*. Walls were sometimes faced with rough-cast (a mixture of lime and gravel) of varying quality; Bait Hanina, Lifta and Majdal Fadil were three of the locations which specialised in its production.

Lead was used for the outer cladding of domes, but far more sparingly than in the Ottoman buildings of Anatolia; as an imported item, it was expensive, and required the services of a specialist. All seven of the Ottoman buildings which use it for their domes are situated in the Haram, a statistic which speaks for itself.

The other two common substances used for specialised aspects of the construction process were iron and wood. Iron was employed principally for nails, which were sometimes heated, but also for wedges and for such fittings as latches, hinges, door-knockers and locks. Wood was the obvious material for balconies, oriel windows, shutters, doors and window frames, and of course scaffolding.

9.4 Vaulting

The dome and the vault were the common currency of the architects of Ottoman Jerusalem; the first and abiding impression of these buildings is their curvilinearity. Apart from structures which of their very nature exclude the dome, such as the *mastaba*s and two-dimensional *sabil*s, virtually every Ottoman monument in the city has a dome. The small scale of most Ottoman architecture in Jerusalem discouraged significant innovations in vaulting technique and even militated against a lively interest in methods of roofing. Indeed, the domes of many of the smaller structures are grossly over-built. Domes were usually diminutive and shallow and so were built without drums, though six of them have 8- or 12-sided drums. The frequency of minor infelicities and adjustments suggests that many masons worked by eye, confident in their ability to muddle through somehow. Cramped and irregular sites generated asymmetrical spaces to be vaulted, and later modifications, additions and rebuildings created still further problems of this kind. Yet the solid competence of these masons ensured that such vaults worked efficiently, even if they were not of drawing-board exactness. It was the norm for the inner surface of vaults and domes to be plastered in plain white. The most popular types were pointed barrel vaults, groin vaults, domes on squinches (though there are only four of these), domes on pendentives and pendentive domes, ribbed saucer domes, cross vaults over rectangular spaces (sometimes with tiercerons), domical vaults, umbrella domes, sail vaults, folded vaults with a hexagonal or octagonal crown or a saucer dome, and star vaults with 12, 16, 20 or 24 points. The North-western Khalwa of Ahmad Pasha even has a dome featuring 32 whorled ribs with 4 pendentives and 8 folded triangles, while Qubbat Yusuf (colour pl. xxiii) has a dome on pendentives whose 38 ribs have a double zigzag frame. The Zawiya al-Muhammadiyya has a domical star vault with a scalloped outer rim, and also a dome on pendentives, whose collar is marked by a continuous open arcade. The interior acquires monumentality from the four arches which carry the dome and whose springing begins just above

83 Qubbat wa Mihrab al-Nabi

84 Qubbat wa Mihrab al-Nabi, *mihrab* and floor *mihrab* in reserve

85 Qubbat wa Mihrab al-Nabi, lower inscription

86 Qubbat wa Mihrab al-Nabi, capital

87 Qubbat al-Khadr, elevation of dome

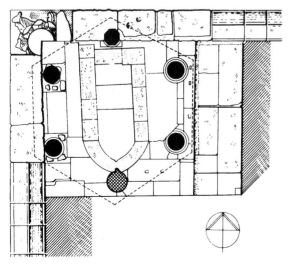

88 Qubbat al-Khadr, ground plan

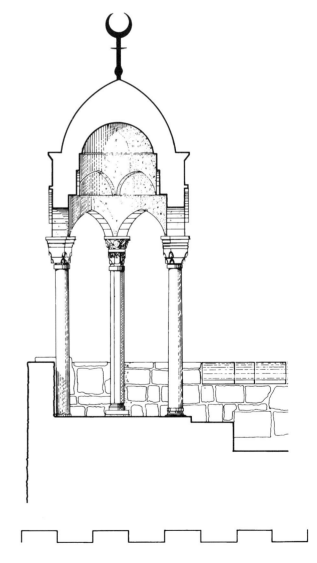

89 Qubbat al-Khadr, section

90 Qubbat al-Arwah, capital

91 Qubbat al-Arwah, capital

92 North-western Khalwa of Ahmad Pasha, capital detail (photograph Joe Rock)

floor level. The Mamluk cell in the north colonnade has a ribbed dome resting on a star-shaped vault whose points touch the springing of the supporting arches, which in turn are of uneven height and thus have their apices follow a rising and falling rhythm. It would be a useful study to collect the terms used by local masons for these very varied forms of roofing; similar work done

in Iraq by Reuther, Langenegger and Herzfeld or in Morocco by Paccard suggests that every form had its own name: 'father of four', 'almond', 'spider's web' or 'four oil lamps'. Naturally the more complex types tended to be those in the most ambitious foundations, such as Khassaki Sultan and the Ribat and Dar of Bairam Jawish. On the other hand, the visible surface of the vault, with its lines picked out sharply in plaster, may not always correspond to what lies beneath, especially in cases where elaborations of the design are executed only shallowly in the plaster. Sometimes, too, the patterns on the underside of these domes are, it seems, merely moulded in the plaster, with spiral, lozenge, and umbrella designs. In a few cases the dome bears external ribs in high relief.

9.5 Capitals and plinths

The readiness of Ottoman architects in Jerusalem to use *spolia* explains the frequency of non-matching columns and capitals in their buildings. The variations in scale are especially intrusive. This suggests that the savings in time and money represented by the re-use in a new setting of existing Islamic capitals and columns counted for more than visual harmony. That said, the simple re-use of earlier capitals, such as basket- and bowl-shaped capitals, is rare. So too is the partial re-use of antique capitals, for example those with foliate scrolls in the upper part of the capital and Ottoman lanceolate niches below. All this is remarkable in view of the many scores of re-used antique capitals in the Dome of the Rock and the Aqsa Mosque, whose presence shows that in the early Islamic period at least there was no inhibition about re-using earlier building material. A typical example of the variety of capitals encountered in a single building is provided by the Qubbat al-Arwah (colour pl. xv). Here some capitals are admittedly similar to each other, but only two are identical; they illustrate basket, *muqarnas* (some fully carved,

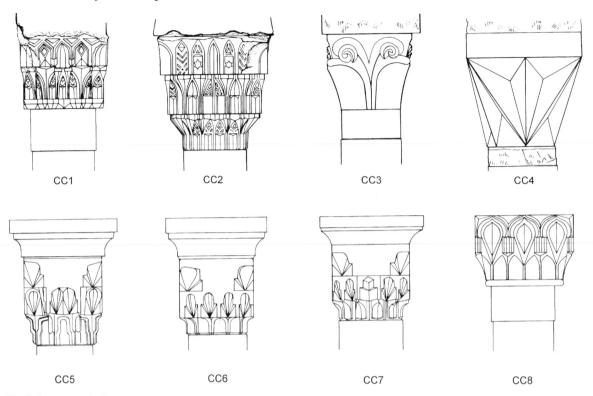

CC1 CC2 CC3 CC4

CC5 CC6 CC7 CC8

93 Column capitals

some with large blank spaces between the *muqarnas* cells, some with plain cells, some whose cells have added internal ornament of vegetal or facetted type, some double-tiered and some triple-tiered) and debased and simplified Corinthian. In one case an extra block of white stone has been inserted below the capital to raise it to the required level. The abacus varies from one capital to the next, but the shafts are identical—which suggests that only the capitals were re-used. Numerous other buildings have three or more varieties of capitals—for example Qubbat al-Nabi, Qubbat al-Khadr and the North-western Khalwa of Ahmad Pasha. Sometimes the irregularity occurs under the umbrella of a broad unity of design, as in the simple planar surfaces of the capitals of the Hujrat Islam Beg. On other occasions, however, the disparity of type is striking. All this suggests, as noted above, an aesthetic untroubled by inconsistencies in what is, after all, traditionally a major element in both the structure and the decoration of a building. It seems that the economic factor was paramount.

It is too early to say whether this easy-going attitude to the choice of capitals was already characteristic of Islamic architecture around the Mediterranean long before Ottoman times. Very little research on the forms of capitals in Islamic architecture has been carried out; there is, for example, no study devoted entirely to Ottoman capitals. This is a pity, for their variety is remarkable. Perhaps the easy availability of antique models in the great Islamic shrines of the city—which, despite the fact of their re-use, were nevertheless sanctified by their Islamic context and thus became suitable models to be copied—made them the natural source of inspiration for the general layout of the standard Ottoman capital. That typical Ottoman capital can be explained quite naturally as a schematised and abstracted version of the successive tiers of foliation in a Corinthian column. The space created by two half-leaves and the meeting-points of their tips resolves itself into a pointed niche which in turn becomes an element integrated into a *muqarnas* system. Similar forms are known in the capitals of late Ottoman Baghdad. Even the volutes of a Corinthian capital may be recognised, much reduced and denatured, in those capitals whose uppermost tier has a middle section which is empty, leaving elaborately carved corners, or conversely is crammed with ornament and leaves the corners quite plain. In both types the ghost of the classical volute can be sensed. It is an instructive example of how Islamic craftsmen understood and re-interpreted the classical heritage, and it is no less revealing even though the model was at that time more than a thousand years old. The sense of natural growth which permeates the classical original has been replaced by a love for regular repetitive pattern; there is variety enough, but each pattern is confined by its niche and cannot develop freely. In similar fashion, the essential three-dimensionality and spatial freedom of the Corinthian capital is toned down to such a degree that the volumes of these Ottoman capitals are compressed, even imprisoned, and thereby lose that suggestion of burgeoning life so appropriate to vegetal ornament. This Ottoman vegetal ornament is rigidly geometricised—for example, the treatment of the cypress motif—and it is not suffered to stray beyond the boundaries set for it. Even the sense of interpenetrating levels which makes classical foliate capitals so lifelike is ironed out so as to separate each tier from the one above or below it. Accordingly it is not surprising that some capitals display a clear hierarchy in their visual vocabulary, with a steady growth in complexity of ornament from the lowest to the topmost tier. Often a heavily ornamented level is set against a plain surface, such as a dosseret.

Basically the interest of Ottoman capitals resides in the experiments made with the *muqarnas* form, and this motif can be studied in the major Ottoman centres of Istanbul and Edirne as well as in provincial contexts. The *muqarnas* motif is not confined to the capital, but sometimes takes over the entire impost, as in some of the *sabils*. When the variations undergone by this familiar motif are closely analysed, they prove to be very close to

each other, but their sculptors managed to make them look different by various means. One was to alternate plain fields for the individual cells with vegetal (e.g. almond or cypress shapes) or geometric infill for them. Another was to contrast a richly carved upper structure for the capital with a plain lower one, or vice versa. Yet another was to leave the central upper portion of the capital plain. Occasionally the *muqarnas* theme is confined to chamfered corner cells. Other and somewhat aberrant types include open papyrus capitals, globular capitals with scalloped bases, *jeux d'esprit* that combine the Ionic with the palm leaf capital, and capitals with plunging angular folded planes, a form possibly inspired by the folded vaults so popular in Ottoman Jerusalem. The abstract palmette that so often features in the upper tier of *muqarnas* capitals has been interpreted as an open 'Hand of Fatima' and could thus partake of the talismanic and apotropaic significance of that motif, which is so popular in the folk art of Palestine. Perhaps the location of such a powerful image in the upper tier of a capital might be thought to be slightly incongruous, but since the purpose of capitals is to carry the superstructure of a building, the protective symbolism of this image would not be unduly misplaced. The abacus is often strongly emphasised, often with an intermediate *cyma recta* or torus moulding. The latter two mouldings are standard in plinths too, but *muqarnas* and basket designs (the latter probably in re-use) are also encountered there. Corbel brackets, for example on minarets, often use the same kind of vocabulary as *muqarnas* capitals.

9.6 Arches

Since so many arches in these buildings are disproportionately large in relation to the buildings in which they appear, they are a key element in the local architectural vocabulary. Such a wide range of arch types was in use during the Ottoman period in Jerusalem that no one type could be termed

94 The Citadel of Jerusalem, mosque—general view looking south-west

standard. The varieties include round or hemispherical, slightly pointed, four-centred, lancet, ogee, trefoil, equilateral, transverse and depressed arches. Relieving arches of various profiles and with voussoirs of consistently odd, never even, numbers are especially popular. Segmental arches, often stilted, shouldered and flat-topped, are repeatedly found crowning the niches of *sabil*s, and the horseshoe form turns up occasionally, though the return is much less pronounced than in Maghribi and Spanish architecture. These multifarious arch forms acquire extra visual interest by the use of two-colour voussoirs and by various mouldings, sometimes as many as six per arch, including gadrooning. On occasion the keystone stands out by virtue of its rhomboidal shape (which may take several forms), or because it breaks the contour of the arch, or is flanked by smaller voussoirs, or thanks to the carved medallion which it bears. All these arches are of stone masonry.

9.7 Stonework

This stonework repays close attention. It is noticeable that subsequent repairs have frequently disfigured these walls, especially in that later repointing has tended to enlarge the apparent width of the joints and thus to blur the previously sharp edges of the stonework. This may seem a

95 Muqarnas niche decorating bevelled edge, corner of al-Zawiya al-Qadiriyya (photograph Joe Rock)

small detail, but it is enough to transform a wall and to blunt its sense of mass. Over-lavish use of mortar also serves to mask how often stones were cut precisely to fit some irregularity in the wall. A brief look at any one of the façades of the North-eastern Khalwa of Ahmad Pasha is enough to reveal that the masons used stones of many different dimensions and deliberately exploited this variety to add life to the wall. There are sufficient examples of the transgression of the main horizontal masonry courses to indicate that these breaks in rhythm, too, were deliberate. The eye is not allowed to dismiss the wall as a piece of mechanically accurate coursing made up of blocks of equal size with regular vertical and horizontal accents. Thus stones of exceptionally large size are framed by others which are exceptionally small. The rising joints zigzag unpredictably along the vertical axis. Nor are the differences in stonework confined to size and colour; texture is an equally significant factor. Thus the extreme smoothness of marble—particularly the grey marble used for lintels and sills, whose natural horizontal graining emphasises this tactile quality—contrasts with the pitted surface of the bulk of the stonework. Rustication was not part of the repertoire of the 16th-century Palestinian stonemason, but the outer surface of some stones is worked with such deliberate roughness that some sculptural effect seems to have been intended. Some of these stones are pock-marked or pitted, others veined, yet others relatively smooth. Thus the variable surface texture of the stones becomes a significant element in the overall impression of a given façade. Rustication is, as it happens, employed in the hall of the Zawiya al-Qadiriyya, but since it is found only there (and on the Dar al-'Adl) it seems likely that it dates from some time other than the rest of the building.

An assured stonework technique is the key to this architecture. Stonework can also have wider implications. Thus the different size of the blocks and the method of stonecutting employed on them sometimes has dating implications. For instance, the presence of different stonework at the lower level in many *khalwa*s suggests that many of these monuments are mere superstructures to earlier buildings which respected the emptiness of the upper platform. In that case it would have been the location of these earlier buildings that dictated that of the Ottoman *khalwa*s. No studies detailed enough to establish dating criteria on the basis of tools used, stone sizes and treatment of surface have yet been carried out. Nevertheless, it is plain that for much of the Ottoman period local fashion preferred a pitted surface to smooth ashlar, though sometimes a compromise was effected whereby the two types of surface were juxtaposed for greater contrast. Thus marginal drafting is employed for the outer edges as a frame for the roughly finished square or rectangular central area. The resultant cloisonné appearance has parallels in earlier Ottoman architecture, for example at Bursa, where—following Byzantine precedent—brick was used to frame stone blocks. In late Ottoman times the technique of rustication was introduced, presumably from Europe; the façade of the Dar al-'Adl is a good example.

It would, as shown above, be wrong to characterise Ottoman masonry technique as even. The wall of the bakery at Khassaki Sultan shows stones with a wide range of sizes and of smoothness; some are heavily, some lightly pitted, and there is no pattern to where these variations occur, nor to where blocks are slightly recessed into the wall. Occasionally a course of narrow horizontal blocks breaks up the wall, or long and short blocks are juxtaposed. By such means the wall itself is animated. Similarly, stone blocks with a smooth surface are sometimes used as quoins to mark the edges of a façade in contradistinction to the roughly-textured stone blocks which make up most of the exterior. Nor are these textures themselves always consistent. The stones of the Khalwat al-Dajani have several different types of dressing—one variety is roughly facetted and betrays the use of a pointed chisel—and this suggests that they were not quarried together but were in secondary use. Special care was taken with the external cladding of domes, for which stones of a uniform size were selected, as the roofscape of Dar Bairam Jawish shows. The stones used in this fashion to 'pave' the exterior of a dome were laid so that their largest surface area was visible. Nevertheless, the tiny size of the stones used for so many Ottoman buildings implies that speed and cheapness of construction were paramount factors. 'Big' in this context is 40 x 192 cm, as in the Madrasa of Ahmad Pasha. Moreover, ashlar masonry, even in the buildings of higher quality, served only as a facing for much rougher masonry. Indeed, the Madrasa of Ahmad Pasha uses plastered rubble for the area behind the façade—a 'cheap and cheerful' solution for surfaces not intended for normal public view. A more standard solution for private as well as public buildings in Ottoman Jerusalem, however, was to sandwich a rubble and plaster mix between an inner and outer layer of dressed stone. The total thickness was usually about 75 cm, corresponding to the Turkish *arsun*, which meant that Ottoman walls tended to be substantially thinner than Mamluk ones, which may explain the Ottoman reliance on buttresses. The outer surface was plastered with lime wash, a solution commonly found in the eastern Mediterranean from Tunisia to Greece irrespective of the dominant religious affiliation of the area concerned.

9.8 Doors and windows

Given the prevailing sobriety of Ottoman architecture in Jerusalem, the special attention paid to doors and windows is particularly striking. Clearly these were intended to be the major accents of a façade—and where the components of a decorative vocabulary are few, it becomes all the more necessary to use them with discrimination. A wide range of lintels is employed for both doors and windows. Flat lintels may consist of a simple horizontal stone beam, often singled out from the surrounding masonry by its smoothness and by its different colour and

material—for example, marble. Or they may be treated as a separate block which, by virtue of its greater size, breaks the regular rhythm of the horizontal coursing into which it is set. But they often stand out by means of joggled bi-coloured voussoirs, usually employing mirror symmetry; a favourite theme here is a lamp-shaped motif, perhaps suggesting the religious function of the building. Other lintels are emphasised by the tapering stepped blocks at their centres, or by the flaring or irregular cut of their constituent blocks. This constant variation in the shape of the voussoirs bears witness to the inexhaustible ingenuity of the local stone-masons, and—quite apart from its effect within its immediate context—it confers a consistent visual interest on a succession of such subtly differentiated façades, most notably in the *khalwa*s bordering the Haram. Sometimes a single or double shallow relieving arch, itself perhaps in two-tone masonry or bearing a carved medallion, surmounts the lintel. The arches of the door or window may exhibit some of these characteristics.

It is not surprising that an architectural style that developed in a crowded urban context should rely so heavily on ways of accentuating the street façade. Many devices to this end had been developed by the Mamluks, but under the Ottomans other original features also evolved. Among them the oriel window deserves special mention. Essentially a combination of balcony and window, and situated high up on the outer façade, it was not only a source of light but also gave the inhabitants of a house an excellent vantage point from which to view the street without being observed themselves. The balcony itself may be of stone or wood, and above it may be as many as five windows on the same level (Dar Muhtadi). Many windows were fitted with iron grilles which not only served to modulate the light that entered a room but also served to articulate a façade. The rectilinear grid of these grilles echoed but did not exactly replicate the coursing of the masonry surrounding them, and thus ensured a consistent

96 Khalwat Sadanat al-Haram, stonework details

97 Khalwat Sadanat al-Haram, stonework details

98 Khalwat Sadanat al-Haram, stonework details

99 Khalwat Sadanat al-Haram, stonework details

100 North-eastern Khalwa of Ahmad Pasha, detail of north façade

101 North-eastern Khalwa of Ahmad Pasha, detail of north façade, detail of stonework

visual impression. Sometimes the window is framed by quoins, or a broad horizontal lintel may crown it. This suggestion of a boundary may be heightened by the sparing use of *ablaq* masonry or of joggled voussoirs.

In the case of windows, which in the upper parts of a façade were often round or disposed in pairs, it is not the treatment of arch or lintel that is visually decisive, but its surroundings, and especially its superstructure. The ensemble of which the window is the centrepiece comprises a narrow recessed vertical panel. Apart from a richly moulded frame, the window itself is apt to be flanked by quoins alternating with stone blocks

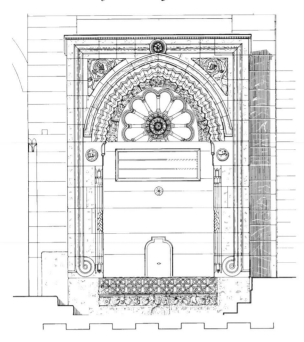

102 Sabil Bab al-Silsila, elevation

103 Sabil al-Wad, elevation

of a different colour or texture. Above the window proper an elaborate multi-tiered design unfolds, in which contrasting colours of stone, joggled voussoirs, glazed blue faience insets, carved roundels, medallions and stars, flat *muqarnas* panels and a stalactite cornice may all play a part. Eight-pointed star windows are a local specialty.

Another local trademark is the preference for paired depressed rounded openings immediately above the lintel or at the base of it, rather like eyebrows. They flank its central axis. They could be regarded as relieving arches. Sometimes, however, they are not open at all, but merely incised. This motif gradually acquires a momentum of its own, for it becomes ever longer and transforms itself into a continuous undulating motif that plays with triangular and semi-circular shapes in turn, often crowned by a central foliate motif. Eventually it blossoms into a pair of hipped, undulating curlicues which—despite their diminutive scale—are enough to break up the ponderous mass of the lintel area.

The apices of ventilation slits offered another fruitful field for experiment. They may take the form of pointed, trefoil or simple ogee arches, but it was the latter profile which was taken as a point of departure for creating numerous stylish and playful forms. These variations on a theme include some extravagant zigzags in bold flourishes and curlicues which never quite break the discipline of the arch. Sometimes a *fleur-de-lis* motif crowns the whole confection. The square, circular and stellar openings for ventilation, which themselves often enclose further radial designs, also invigorate otherwise empty façades.

9.9 Pottery screens

Often the bridges or private pathways over the streets—of which more than two dozen survive—are lightened by being constructed over tiers of hollow baked clay pipes whose openings are so disposed as to form triangular patterns. These pottery screens also serve to modulate light filtering into the areas behind them. Such pottery walls are also employed as screens marking off the top of courtyards and demarcating boundaries at parapet level. They are not peculiar to Jerusalem but are a feature of pre-modern Palestinian architecture, as

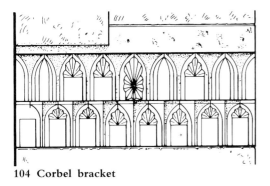

104 Corbel bracket

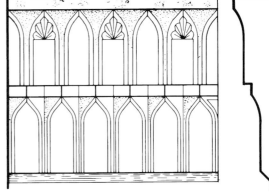

105 Corbel bracket

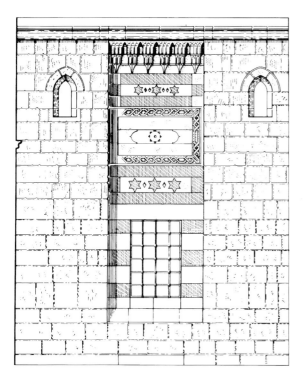

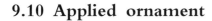

106 Windows

at Ramla. Similar forms were also common in late Ottoman Baghdad.

9.10 Applied ornament

It was standard practice to reserve the best decoration for key locations; thus the Madrasa of Ahmad Pasha displays more decoration on the *qibla* side than elsewhere. But of course applied

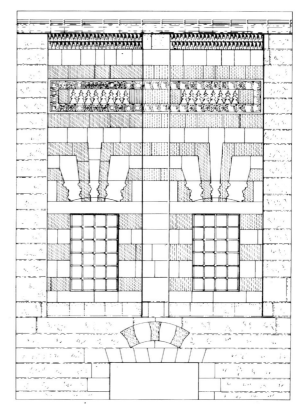

ornament clearly has financial dimensions, and in view of the obviously limited budget for most Ottoman buildings in Jerusalem it is not surprising that most of them rely principally on the aesthetic effect of good-quality stonework for their appearance. But that stonework is rarely monotonous. At the simplest level, it is animated, as already discussed, by changes in the size or texture of the stones themselves. The next stage is

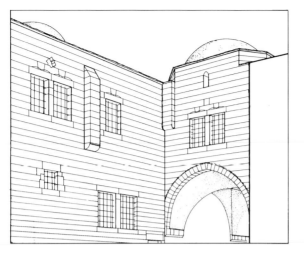

107 Corbelled buttresses

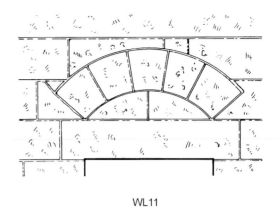

WL11

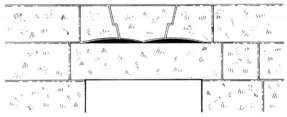

WL12

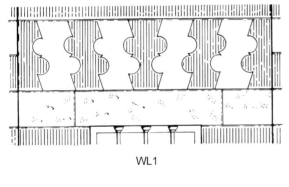

WL1

WL2

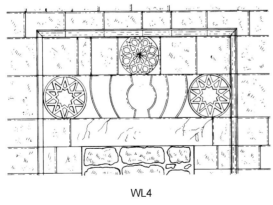

WL4

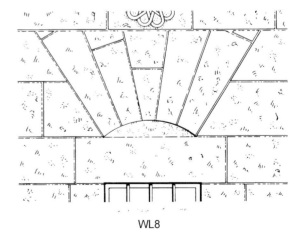

WL8

108 Window lintels/arches

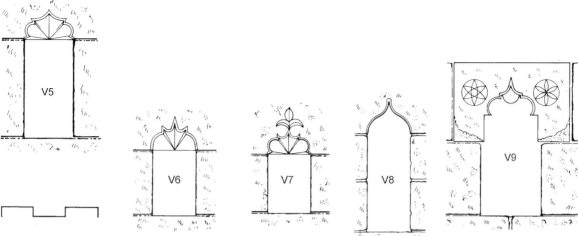

109 Ventilation slits

marginally more complex: blank recessed panels sometimes enliven a façade in an understated way. Nevertheless, the modesty of this decorative accent is in striking contrast to, say, Mamluk modes. In somewhat more ambitious vein, the arch over a window may have a blank arch of similar size and profile above it—this would also strengthen the arch. Conversely, arches or lintels may feature stones of flaring or bevelled cut, or set diagonally, thereby emphasising the window or lintel as an articulating device on the façade. Another way of attaining the same end is to use blocks of stone cut into triangular, tapering or rhomboidal shapes to break the even coursing of a wall. These deliberate variations in the stonework are merely a more ostentatious way of animating the surface than the normal practice of irregularly spaced horizontal and vertical jointing in the masonry. All

these devices—and related examples could be multiplied—are rooted in an immemorial local tradition of stonework and in an instinctive appreciation of its aesthetic potential.

But the entire dimension of colour (see below) is much reduced, for no painted plaster survives and the only colour is that of the stone masonry itself, which is red, ochre and white; the latter has sometimes weathered to grey but often has a creamy tint. The black hue of much of this stonework is also not its natural colour; it has various causes, among them the effect of water, wind, shadow or fungal growth. The resultant contrast of surfaces can be quite startling: thus the Hujra of Islam Beg has a main façade of predominantly white stone and a rear façade of predominantly black stone (colour pls. xiv and xvii), all apparently due to weathering. It should be remembered that these visual effects would have been less marked in times when the lime wash covering the outer surface of a building was regularly renewed.

A very few buildings, notably the *sabils*, display varied and complex ornament. Qubbat Yusuf (1681) is another good example (colour pl. xxiii). This is a smaller building than the Qubbat Yusuf Agha by the same patron, but much more richly decorated. Why? The reason may be that it is on the upper terrace, where space is much more limited, and where a bigger building that might

110 Carved stone decoration detail on building close to Nabi Da'ud

111 North-western Khalwa of Ahmad Pasha, detail of west window

upstage the Dome of the Chain, let alone the Dome of the Rock, was excluded. But the very choice of the upper rather than the lower terrace (where the Qubbat Yusuf Agha is located) created an extra prestige and aura of sanctity for the building and made lavish decoration all the more appropriate. Indeed, this was the best available way of expressing extra importance—size was not an option. The inclusion of an inscribed Ayyubid plaque gives the *qubba* an ancient pedigree and, as van Berchem argued, extra prestige.

Perhaps the favourite decorative theme of Ottoman architects in Jerusalem was the *muqarnas*. It turns up in all kinds of guises. Thus Sabil Birkat al-Sultan has a tympanum with three tiers of *muqarnas*, each one differentiated from the others; this is a highly developed use of this theme. Sometimes, as at Sabil Bab al-'Atm, the *muqarnas* is even used upside down. At the Zawiya al-Qadiriyya, as at Maqam al-Nabi Da'ud, a shallow *muqarnas* niche just above eye level marks the

junction where two external façades meet at right angles: a modest but elegant boundary indicator. The Maktab of Bairam Jawish has on its first-floor elevation a band of ten and a half triangular lancet panels of *muqarnas* type, all different. The *muqarnas* also serves a useful role as a support for the gallery of local minarets.

The range of mouldings is somewhat limited. The denticulated frieze used at the Qubbat al-Khadr to outline (and over-emphasise) the main arches on the external façade recurs in several other buildings of the period of Sulaiman and later in Jerusalem: Maqam al-Nabi Da'ud, the minaret of the Citadel, Sabil Bab al-Silsila and Sabil Bab al-Nazir. Other mouldings are more or less accurate versions of such classical types as the cavetto, *cyma recta* or *cyma reversa*. Occasionally they are serrated or bear applied ornament such as diaper-work. Roll and billet mouldings were also popular, while volutes as thick as organ-pipes frame several *sabils*. Braided and chevron mouldings were also popular.

Cornices, too, follow set patterns. That on the Qubbat al-Khadr consists of a miniature arcade with a leaf form in the field of each arch. Another common form for cornices was a *muqarnas* system, whether single- or multi-tiered, or a band of facetted triangles or denticulations. The formula customarily involves a long or short perpendicular plane at the top of the cornice, with convex, concave or indented planes immediately below. Some cornices simply consist of billet, roll or ogee mouldings. Still other buildings have vestigial or abruptly interrupted cornices, and some have none at all. This is of a piece with the determined simplicity of the local style in Ottoman times.

In contradistinction to Mamluk practice, which favoured bold accents such as large-scale *muqarnas* compositions in portals, large panels of geometric ornament, lengthy inscription bands, fully three-dimensional *muqarnas* compositions and the lavish use of *ablaq* on façades, Ottoman ornament is delicate but parsimonious in its placing. This ensures that what ornament there is can exert maximum impact. Much use is made of stone roundels with carved geometric (often stellar) designs, sometimes enriched by stylised flowers and rosettes, a treasury of ornament which has been lovingly chronicled by Sylvia Auld. These roundels are used as grace notes rather than as a regular element in the mason's vocabulary. In this they conform to the taste for the sparing use of decorative accents. Their designs frequently recall the repertoire of 16th-century Iznik pottery, though of course their emphasis on the blossom alone rather than the complete flower excludes the naturalism which could be such a hallmark of that ceramic tradition. A similar fascination with different types of flowers characterises contemporary Ottoman book painting, as the *Süleymanname* shows. The fullest collection of these roundels is to be found on the city walls, a favoured location for such roundels elsewhere in the Islamic world. Some 120 survive on the walls of Jerusalem (though the estimates vary considerably). Some may also have been intended to bear a symbolic

meaning, notably in the frequent repetition of the *khatam Sulaiman*, the Seal of Solomon, perhaps a graceful allusion to the builder of those walls. That motif has a long history as an apotropaic symbol, and as such would have been well suited for use

112   **Citadel of Jerusalem, medallion above** *mihrab*

113 **Roof of upper room of Bait Mamluk, constructed** *c.* **1870, showing the ventilated parapet walls**

114 Al-ʿImara al-ʿAmira, detail of south portal
(photograph Joe Rock)

115 Roundel with *khatam sulaiman* on interior façade
of Herod's Gate (Bab al-Zahra)

116 Roundel with 4-part *rumi* motif

117 Detail of carved stone roundel on Dar Bairam
Jawish (photograph Joe Rock)

on the walls which protected the Holy City.
Roundels in the form of star polygons clustering
at the key sites of the city gates may also have been
intended as talismans, a function suggested by the
way that they were used in Mamluk times. Other
roundels could have had a religious significance:
the Habsburg ambassador to the Sublime Porte,
Ogier de Busbecq, notes that the Ottomans 'believe
that the rose sprang from the sweat of Mahomet.'
It is well to remember that the tradition of

decorating Islamic city walls with signs of power—
whether secular or religious—and of personalised
possession was an ancient one, stretching from
Muslim Spain to India. Symbolic motifs vied with
inscriptions to broadcast such messages, as can be
seen in Seville and Granada, Rabat and Marrakesh,
Cairo and Damascus, Aleppo and Amida, and as
far east as Herat and Delhi. Stone bosses, also
strategically placed at intervals along the walls of
Jerusalem and occasionally within the gates, and
for which parallels in Ottoman manuscripts can
also be cited, complement the roundels and, like
them, were probably painted or even gilded so as
to increase their visual impact. These carefully
placed nuggets of intense decoration served to

bring the walls to life but may also, in addition to their possible apotropaic, personalised or religious function have been intended to place a recognisably Ottoman stamp on the city and even to sanctify it. It has even been suggested that, within the city, they may have served as markers for the way to the Haram al-Sharif. One should remember, too, that none of these functions or meanings are mutually exclusive, and that the very power of symbols rests in part on their capacity to suggest several meanings simultaneously. Be that as it may, the spectacle of these ornamented walls must have been visually striking. An anonymous but celebrated Venetian painting of the very late 15th century in the Louvre, *The Reception of the Ambassadors*, purports to depict a scene outside the walls of Damascus and records the environment of this ceremony in meticulous detail. It represents those walls prinked out with technicolour Mamluk blazons and thus offers a broadly contemporary parallel to how the walls of Jerusalem might have looked in the 1540s.

The roundels are by no means confined to the walls; some 29 occur in the 'Imarat Khassaki Sultan, including an open flower motif which significantly recurs, as Sylvia Auld notes, on the complex of Hasseki Sultan Hürrem in Istanbul and may operate as some kind of personal blazon in these buildings. A further nine roundels occur in the Dar of Bairam Jawish and there are five in the North-eastern Khalwa of Ahmad Pasha. Among their favoured locations in these and other buildings are the spaces within each of the lower lobes of a trilobed arch and at the centre of the tympanum of a *sabil*. More generally, they serve to highlight spandrels, to mark or crown the apices of arches, and to emphasise the key central and outer points of the entablature crowning doors and windows. Similar forms, but pierced, also serve as windows.

A few examples of stone sculpture also deserve mention. Of outstanding interest in this respect is the remarkably varied series of finials which crown the domes of buildings on the Haram;

they are substantially rarer elsewhere in the city, which suggests that they connoted an extra degree of sanctity. They make much play of the superposition of successive simple but powerful geometric shapes: shafts, cubes, rectangles, ovals, circles, octagons both regular and irregular, abaci and various bevelled forms, the whole usually crowned by a crescent with horizontal or pointed ends, by cones or by rings open at their apex. The Sabil of Mustafa Agha has hexagonal columns, of which four sides are decorated (all differently) and two plain (colour pl. xxvii), and the same system is found at the *mihrab* of the Iwan of Sultan Muhammad II. The Khalwat Parwiz has a window crowned by a triangle whose lobed sides enclose a thicket of dense floral ornament executed in precision carving. Thus the capacity for applied ornament in stone was there, as in contemporary Damascus and Aleppo, ready to be called forth by the right kind of patronage. But for the most part decoration was restricted, in David Myres' luminous phrase, to 'a light touch on a heavy structure'.

What of the dimension of colour? This has many aspects. In general, it is much reduced, for no painted plaster survives and the only colour is that of the stone masonry itself. The nature of the local stone is therefore crucial. Its colour, as already noted above, is far from consistent, varying as it does from a blackish grey to off-white. Often quite marked variations occur on a single block of stone. Sometimes it takes on a mottled brownish tinge; in many cases it has weathered to black. The masons proved adept at varying the colour harmonies of their façades and creating accents at specific or random intervals by the placing of a single lighter or darker block, or by varying the colour as well as the tonality. The patchwork result bears a startling resemblance to certain types of modern abstract art. Grey, white, red and yellow stone used in contrasting colours can be interpreted as a continuation of Mamluk *ablaq*, although it is distinctly different, for example in its much more random application. Moreover, the fashion for true *ablaq* was definitively discarded in early Ottoman

118 Star-polygonal device on carved stone roundel in 'Aqabat al-Takiyya

119 Star-polygonal with 10 points, flanking the Damascus Gate

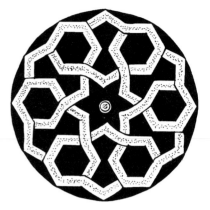

120 Hexagonal geometric interlace—the basic design on a roundel at Jaffa Gate (Bab al-Khalil)

121 A five-petalled device in the south entrance porch to al-'Imara al-'Amira

122 Roundel on the main portal of the Citadel

123 Roundel with naturalistic 'daisy' on 'Tower' 22

124 Variant of the *khatam sulaiman*, near Tancred's Tower

125 Hexagonal geometric interlace on a roundel at Jaffa Gate (Bab al-Khalil)

126 Variant of the *khatam sulaiman*, in the Muslim cemetery

architecture in Jerusalem, possibly in a bid to assert the transfer of power to a new dynasty. Colour contrasts come into their own for the decoration of window frames, *mihrabs*, the fields of blind arches, two-tone or joggled voussoirs—used in lintels as well as in arches—counter-change designs or even simple single or double string courses, arch profiles, keystones, jambs and quoins, as at the North-eastern Khalwa of Ahmad Pasha. The Mihrab of 'Ali Pasha uses four tones: white, grey, red and black, while two-tone marble floors are quite common. Coloured stone or marble, sometimes heightened by the use of tiny blue faience insets in the shapes of stars or triangles, was ideal for the six-pointed star—often known as Solomon's Seal and perhaps intended too as a flattering reference to the great Ottoman sultan himself—which is such a leitmotif on these façades. The masterpiece of such marble compositions is to be found in the door-frame of the ancillary chamber of the North-western Khalwa of Ahmad Pasha, whose beauty lies in its very understatement (see below for a more detailed account). The muted pastel tones set each other off to perfection, and because they are applied in such broad bands the cartouches and stars placed at such intervals along them function as accompaniments to an abstract colour composition rather than as the focus of interest. This is also the role of the square glazed *tesserae* used so sparingly in these buildings; it is perhaps a reflection of the poverty of Ottoman Jerusalem in comparison with, say, Ottoman Damascus that—apart from the very special case of the Dome of the Rock, which represents an intrusion of top-level imperial patronage—the Iznik-style tilework of Damascus is so conspicuously absent. This is truly remarkable, especially as the enormous task of re-tiling the exterior of the Dome of the Rock meant that local workshops were established. Clearly their production was set aside for that building alone. Such tilework as survives elsewhere in the city is not only so rare as to be insignificant, as shown for example by the tiles over the doorway of Maktab

of Bairam Jawish, but of indifferent quality.

Colour is also used somewhat unexpectedly to create *mihrabs* in floors. Sometimes this theme is echoed in the elevation; thus the Qubbat wa Mihrab al-Nabi (colour pl. xxiv) has a diminutive niche with a central red band running through a line of concave cylindrical indentations, a blind arcade, thereby emphasising—and in the same colours—the *qibla* already announced by the Mamluk *mihrab* laid in reserve on the floor. It is not easy to explain the preference for reserved *mihrabs* (*mihrab makhtut fi 'l-ard*), for some of which two- or three-tone marble or stone is used. This is not an Ottoman idea; it was already in use at least in Mamluk times if not earlier. The idea of floor-level, 'inlaid' *mihrabs* finds multiple expressions in the Islamic world, from carpets with rows of *mihrabs* in Turkey, Tunisia and elsewhere to entire pavements with this theme, as at Mazar-i Sharif in Afghanistan. One may suggest that in the Haram al-Sharif this type of *mihrab* was used so as not to encroach too obviously on the more holy monuments all around.

One building alone, already briefly mentioned above, stands out from all the rest for its sovereign assurance in the use of colour: the North-western Khalwa of Ahmad Pasha, datable 1007-9/1598-1601 but appropriately nicknamed 'the Mamluk cell'. Two identical panels survive, one on the east elevation and the other, perfectly preserved, on the east wall of the inner antechamber (colour pl. xx). The chaste and muted splendour of its pastel palette is overwhelming in the confined space of this little room. A peerless sense of interval dictates the balance between lightly and heavily veined stone, between paler and darker accents, between smooth surfaces and corrugated, reversed 'S' patterns, in the immaculately cut and fitted stone. That stone, by turns creamy, reddish, ochre and greyish-blue, is set off by tiny glazed insets in dark blue, grace notes at key locations on and flanking the chord of the doorway. The whole composition breathes a natural affinity with the chromatic potential of the local stone and is rooted in generations of experience with that material, Hence its remarkable smoothness and the sweetness of its joints. There is no finer stonework to be found anywhere in the city.

9.11 *Spolia*

Spolia are part of the stock in trade of the local architects. Indeed, the *sijill*s are full of references to the sale and purchase of ready-made building materials. A *sijill* reference from 1530 indicates that a block of dressed stone fetched a silver piece at that time. Clearly, then, there was no lack of incentive for a thriving trade in these materials to develop. Re-used material came from several sources: whether *spolia* from destroyed buildings, gleanings from ruins or merely fragments from the stock kept by local masons. The prevalence of *spolia* is not surprising because Jerusalem was such a rich quarry for buildings of pre-Ottoman times, many of them non-Muslim and inadequately protected from despoliation. In a few cases, such as Sabil Bab al-Silsila, a foreign origin is manifest: here a truncated Crusader rose window is crammed into the tympanum (colour pl. xxxii). The design of this *sabil*, with its unmistakably Christian aspect turned to Muslim uses, was, incidentally, copied in the course of the 18th century in the guise of the portal of the Masjid 'Umar, situated just next to the Holy Sepulchre—this time even more probably for purposes of polemic. At the Sabil Bab al-Nazir a Crusader arch and Crusader columns with a plaited central braid sit rather uneasily alongside Ottoman *muqarnas* work (colour pl. xxxi), while Sabil Bab al-'Atm uses a non-Ottoman chevron motif, and the Zawiya al-Naqshbandiyya has a chevron arch. It remains an open question why these *spolia* (and motifs of non-Ottoman origin) were such a marked feature of the *sabil*s founded by Sultan Sulaiman. In any event, this use of *spolia* follows precedents set in Nurid, Ayyubid and Mamluk times, as illustrated by the antique patinas (sigma-shaped

tables) re-used in 12th-century Syrian mosques and *madrasa*s; the Turba al-Nahawiyya on the Haram; Christian columns in Maghribi architecture; Byzantine capitals in the Aqsa Mosque; and—most eye-catching of all—the Gothic portal of the church of St John at Acre, which was incorporated into the funerary *madrasa* of Sultan al-Malik al-Nasir Muhammad in Cairo. Nor were such *spolia* confined to the *sabil*s. The Qubbat Yusuf boasts not only a chevron and gadrooned arch but also two Crusader columns and capitals (colour pl. xxiii). Indeed, it is a hotchpotch of borrowed elements, and shows how variously therefore Crusader *spolia* were incorporated into the Islamic repertoire. A triumphalist intention here, though politically quite outdated, is possible in this case because the concentration of foreign material is so strong and because this aedicule is close to the Nahawiyya, which suggests an Ottoman sensitivity to making the same point as that building and in the same visual language.

Often enough, however, the *spolia* carry no extra charge of triumphalism. They may not even be intended to suggest continuity. Sometimes the rarity of a material is sufficient reason for its re-use in a new context, as in the red stone used for floor *mihrab*s, or even the red granite at the foot of the south column in the Qubbat al-Khadr, which serves as a crude *mihrab* in itself. More often, it is simply a matter of using the available dressed stone as seems best to the mason on the spot. Such masons, it seems, were not attuned to architectural proprieties. Thus the

127 North-western Khalwa of Ahmad Pasha, detail of capital re-used as column base

Qubbat Yusuf re-employs column bases as capitals. Similarly, in the Hujrat Islam Beg, the shafts are in secondary use (colour pl. xvii), which implies the desire to save money and an indifference to appearances even on the Haram. These are jerry-made columns, made up of slightly uneven blocks, and they carry disproportionately huge capitals. Columns are of different height, diameter and colour in a single building; sometimes a structure with only eight capitals will have no two that are identical. This readiness to use second-hand material betrays a certain indifference to the visual aspect of a building, which in turn may help to explain the gross asymmetries and disparities which disfigure façades that in other respects display exemplary craftsmanship, such as the four façades, each one quite different from the next, of the North-western Khalwa of Ahmad Pasha (colour pls. xix, xxi, xxix, xxx). Such details bespeak not only a lack of coherence, a lack of vision about the project as a whole, but also an absence of oversight.

The structural dimension of using *spolia* should not be forgotten. Very often metal bands are applied around the columns. This is not only a sure sign that the elements thus joined had not been carved to be used together, but also suggests that the structure was perceived to be weak, perhaps even damaged, in which case such bands could serve to conceal the fact. They may also be a precaution against earthquake. Further uses for metal clamps are to be seen in the Qubbat al-Arwah, where rivets are employed to join some of the blocks forming the raised border of the floor and a metal tie-beam has been inserted at springing level (colour pl. xv).

Stone has always been the traditional building material in Jerusalem, and the labour of dressing it means that whenever it is possible to employ re-used stones, builders will do so. The clearance of debris from the Haram in the 1550s

128 Sabil Mustafa Agha, inscription panel

made available a great mass of worked stones, and some of them can be located in such foundations as Khassaki Sultan.

9.12 Inscriptions

The role of inscriptions in the architecture of Ottoman Jerusalem is curiously minimal, especially in comparison with its importance in Mamluk times. They are almost uniformly modest in their location, panel size, length and tone. It is too early to state definitively that a standard Ottoman local form for inscription panels evolved. The necessary detailed research remains to be done. Nevertheless, some continuity from earlier periods is quickly recognisable. In the Masjid al-Saif, the inscription in the name of Sulaiman continues Mamluk modes, especially the Qa'it Bay style in its use of *naskhi*, not *thulth*, and its uneven tripartite design. Further noteworthy features here are the thick forms of the letters and the unusual positioning of this inscription at the keystone of the *mihrab* arch. Equally unusual is the thick and chunky *naskhi* inscription on the Kursi Sulaiman. Most panels are in marble (colour pl. xxv) but a few use limestone. While a rectangular format for inscription plaques—another Mamluk heritage—was standard, the octagonal form was also known. Such panels were lightly ornamented with rounded corners or a plain fillet border; lobed cartouches, some of them richly ornamented with flowers, branches and leaves of various kinds, are also known. Sometimes these panels are recessed. A few inscriptions, including those with a date, are in Ottoman Turkish, and sometimes both languages are used together. Many inscriptions are in Arabic poetry, and it is standard practice to give the date by chronogram as well as in figures. Most inscriptions are carved in relief; only two are incised. Two buildings only—the Qubbat Yusuf and the Qubbat Yusuf Agha—have two dated inscription panels of similar content.

129 Qubbat Yusuf Agha, inscription

The content of these inscriptions has not received separate study as a body of connected material. Not surprisingly, however, there are references or allusions to the special sanctity of Jerusalem, to the hope of paradise, to the performance of *ziyara* or to prophets who have a particular link with the city. Thus an inscription from Kursi Sulaiman quotes from the Qur'anic story of the encounter between Solomon and Bilqis, the Queen of Sheba, and thereby confirms that its popular name today accurately reflects the original purpose of the building, namely to commemorate Solomon. It is noticeable that the Ibn Nammar family, for all that it continued to be prominent in architectural matters from generation to generation, does not figure at all in the epigraphic record, although some of them (especially Husain ibn Nammar) were certainly among the notables of their time. Indeed, as already noted, were it not for the Shari'a Court records, we would know nothing at all about them.

9.13 Summary

Any analysis of the architectural style of Ottoman Jerusalem must take account of the way that these buildings are concentrated within narrow parameters. The emphasis on the *khalwa*, the commemorative aedicule and the *sabil*; the fact that so much of this architecture is Haram-related and is indeed located there; and the fact that almost everything of quality was erected in the first century of Ottoman power—all these restrictions result in this architecture being of somewhat limited scope and relevance. The absence of major mosques, *madrasa*s, mausolea and *khan*s has already been remarked (Chapter 6.1) and it points in the same direction. A particular consequence of the close focus on the Haram was that the competition which was the life-blood of the architecture of Mamluk Jerusalem and was allowed relatively free rein because it flourished in the city proper was denied to the Ottomans—work in the Haram had to proceed much more circumspectly.

As it happens, the local style changed remarkably little in the course of the Ottoman period. This in itself is an index of the remoteness of Jerusalem from the fashions which came and went in larger centres. The baroque and rococo elements which transformed later Ottoman architecture elsewhere occur only intermittently, like the rustication on the façade of the Dar al-'Adl. This architecture possessed the virtue of straightforward good manners, expressed in simple forms, clean, consistent, sober stereotomy, a generally uniform colour and material, restrained articulation and parsimonious ornament. Its preferred forms were simple, strong, cubic. These

characteristics, though they may sound rather unexciting, do deserve scrutiny.

Formal inventiveness is not the strong suit of local architects. It is well, however, to remember the modularity of Ottoman architecture, with its unflagging focus on the domed square as the base unit of the design. Thus the architecture of Jerusalem is thoroughly in tune with the spirit of Ottoman architecture generally. That domed square unit recurs repeatedly both in open-plan designs like the so-called Iwan of Mahmud II and in the constricted space of the typical *khalwa* on the Haram terrace. Moreover, its visual impact could vary quite dramatically, not only according to its size but also to whether it was isolated, doubled, or attached to other forms such as the great arcades of the Haram. A popular fashion was to place a multi-domed arched portico in front of one or more domed squares, a formula very popular for small mosques from early Ottoman times onwards. No matter whether the buildings are large or small, the aim of their architects is consistent: to achieve maximum monumentality with minimum means.

10 CONCLUSION

The present study represents the first serious attempt to record the buildings of Ottoman Jerusalem in a concise format. For the same task, but accomplished in a comprehensive manner, the obvious source of reference is *Ottoman Jerusalem, The Living City 1517-1917*. But even those volumes cannot hope to say the last word on any of these buildings, and should rather be regarded as a foundation on which future research can be based. It is now clear, however, that the architecture of Ottoman Jerusalem, which grows so naturally out of the rich Mamluk heritage in the city, and has its own distinctive local character, repays close study. The absence of major buildings of international importance is less significant than the preservation, in largely excellent condition, of an entire pre-modern town. That town is overwhelmingly an Arab one, and to this day it is cherished by its Muslim inhabitants. Written records corroborate oral traditions that many of its distinguished families have been there for centuries. This book owes a great deal to the love which the local Muslims have for Jerusalem, and it is a matter for celebration that the city's heritage of Ottoman buildings has now been recorded in detail in the parent volumes of which this is an offshoot.

The manifold activities of Ottoman architects in Jerusalem, as recorded in the registers of the Shari'a Court, extended far beyond the erection of buildings. These wonderfully detailed documents create a thorough social context for the buildings which brings them vibrantly to life. From these records we can trace in detail how they were built, but in addition to that we learn how they were financed, how they operated from day to day, and how disputes about their condition, function and ownership were handled. In all of this the architects, especially the local Ibn Nammar family, were major players, by turn builders, astute businessmen, investors, managers, surveyors and inspectors, paralegals, valuation experts, estate agents and power brokers. All this evidence, much of it assembled by Yusuf Natsheh and Mahmud Atallah, forces a fundamental re-assessment of the role of the architect in pre-modern Muslim society. So far as the construction side of their profession was concerned, these local architects had inherited from their Mamluk and still earlier predecessors an enviable confidence in the working of the local stone and a keen awareness of its possibilities. In general, their taste was austere, even minimalist, in comparison with Mamluk work. Buildings are often generically akin with their Mamluk counterparts, but have as it were lost their decoration. The beauty of the stonework and the simplicity of the basic forms—arcades, aedicules, domed squares, façades with recessed vertical panels—is allowed to speak for itself. The articulation is pared down to mouldings, capitals, plinths, embrasures and the like, and is consistently set off by expanses of plain stonework.

The Ottomans were the last major Islamic dynasty of international stature to rule Jerusalem. Theirs was by far the most sophisticated and powerful of the late medieval to early modern Islamic states; indeed, in some sense this was the supreme Islamic dynasty. It brought to fruition many trends and ideas which were latent in earlier Islamic polities. It imposed its stamp on much of the Islamic world and for centuries it symbolised that world to the West. The Ottomans are the final link in a chain which, apart from a brief rupture under Crusader rule, stretches back well over a millennium to the beginning of Muslim rule in 638. The Islamic presence, then, is no transient episode; it is fundamental to an understanding of the city, past, present and future. Indeed, despite the evidence of Christian and Jewish presence in the Old City over the centuries, this is a Muslim town through and through. The intrinsically Islamic nature of the physical fabric of the Old City is frequently undervalued and even ignored in the West. It is sometimes demoted in the media to mere local colour. Yet even the most casual and uninformed visitor to the city cannot fail to notice this pervasive Islamic dimension. Most of the fabric which is an integral, tangible part of that dimension is of Ottoman date. Every stone of that fabric is part of a precious heritage and it deserves loving protection.

The buildings of Ottoman Jerusalem are a solid reminder that, alongside the city that enshrines the three monotheistic faiths, over which so many wars have been fought over the millennia, and which for decades now has been the centre of a storm of political controversy, there is another and more down-to-earth Jerusalem. This is the city in which for many centuries Muslim, Christian and Jew have gone about their daily business. That working city cannot, perhaps, rival the glamour,

the numinous resonances and the potent associations cast by the Jerusalem of Solomon, of Jesus, and of Saladin. But it incorporates some of the very fabric of those other, more ancient forerunners of our own days. That Jerusalem is not just an idea; it is a physical reality. It is the Jerusalem which forty generations of Muslims have tended faithfully. Their history is written into these stones. And—to repeat a point made earlier in this book— the architecture presented here accurately represents the nature of the Ottoman city between *c.* 1500 and *c.* 1800, a period which saw the erection of the great majority (some 93 percent) of the buildings described here. This was essentially a Muslim city; and these buildings are the proof of that assertion.

This book, then, is intended as a timely record of an Islamic heritage that is rapidly disappearing in the Middle East. It describes in general terms the public buildings which created a physical context for the lives led in this very special city. They evoke a continuous Islamic presence which has lasted for some fourteen centuries and imprinted itself on the entire urban fabric. It is my hope that this book, and of course much more so its parent volumes, will help to ensure that the Muslim tradition in Jerusalem, alongside those of Christianity and Judaism, is accorded its place in the sun.

MAP OF OTTOMAN JERUSALEM

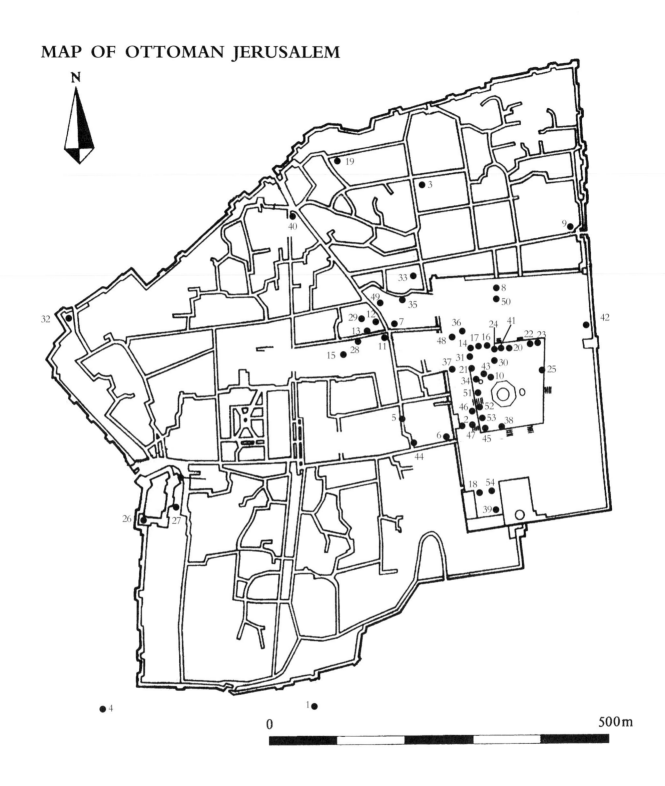

The map shows the locations of the Ottoman monuments. The list on the facing page gives the names of the buildings against the numbers shown on the map.

OTTOMAN JERUSALEM: CATALOGUE OF BUILDINGS

Number	Name and date
1.	Masjid and Minaret al-Nabi Da'ud 930/1524
2.	Sabil Qasim Pasha 933/1527
3.	Minaret and Zawiyat al-Hamra' (al-Khalwatiyya) c.939/1532-3
4.	Sabil Birkat al-Sultan 943/1536
5.	Sabil al-Wad 943/1536
6.	Sabil Bab al-Silsila 943/1537
7.	Sabil Bab al-Nazir 943/1537
8.	Sabil Bab al-'Atm 943/1537
9.	Sabil Bab Sitti Maryam 943/1536-7
10.	Qubbat wa Mihrab al-Nabi 945/1538-9
11.	Ribat Bairam Jawish 947/1540
12.	Maktab Bairam Jawish 947/1540
13.	Dar Bairam Jawish 953/1546
14.	Hujrat Muhammad Amir Liwa' al-Quds 956/1549-50
15.	Al-'Imara al-'Amira (Khassaki Sultan) 959/1552
16.	Khalwat Qitas 967/1559-60
17.	Khalwat Parwiz 967/1559-60
18.	Sabil Bab al-Magharibia (first endowment) 987/1579
19.	Al-Khanqah al-Maulawiyya 995/1586-7
20.	Hujrat Muhammad Agha 996/1588
21.	Hujrat Islam Beg 1002/1593-4
22.	North-Western Khalwa of Ahmad Pasha (Mamluk cell) 1009/1601
23.	North-Eastern Khalwa of Ahmad Pasha 1009/1601
24.	Khalwat Junbalatiyya 1010/1601-2
25.	Madrasat Ahmad Pasha 1013/1604
26.	Mi'dhanat Qal'a (restoration) 1065/1655
27.	Masjid al-Saif (restoration) 1151/1643-4
28.	Al-Madrasa al-Mawardiyya (al-Rasasiyya), first half of 16th century?
29.	Al-Zawiya al-Muhammadiyya, first half of 16th century?
30.	Qubbat al-Arwah, before 1037/1637-8
31.	Qubbat al-Khadr, before 1222/1807
32.	Masjid al-Qaimari 16th century?
33.	Al-Zawiya al-Naqshbandiyya 1033/1623-4
34.	Khalwat Bairam Pasha 1038/1628-9
35.	Al-Zawiya al-Qadiriyya 1043/1633
36.	Sabil wa Mihrab wa Mastabat Sha'lan, (reconstruction) 1037/1627-8
37.	Mihrab 'Ali Pasha 1047/1637-8
38.	Qubbat Yusuf 1092/1681
39.	Qubbat Yusuf Agha 1092/1681
40.	Sabil al-Shurbaji 1097/1685
41.	Odat Arslan Pasha, (restoration) 1109/1697
42.	Kursi Sulaiman, after 1017/1608
43.	Al-Zawiya al-Muhammadiyya (Masjid al-Nabi) 1112/1700-1
44.	Sabil al-Khalidi 1125/1713
45.	Sabil al-Husaini 1137/1724-5
46.	Khalwat al-Dajani 1138/1725-6
47.	Mihrab Ahmad Qullari 1174/1760-1
48.	Sabil Mustafa Agha (al-Budair) 1153/1740-1
49.	Dar al-'Izz 1205/1790-91
50.	Iwan al-Sultan Mahmud II 1233/1817-18
51.	Khalwat Sadanat al-Haram 1222/1807
52.	Khalwat al-Mu'adhdhinin after 1222/1807
53.	South-Western Khalwa 1222/1807
54.	Mihrab wa Mastabat al-Sanaubar, undated
55.	Mastabas and Mihrabs, undated *(not shown on map)*

BIBLIOGRAPHY

The principal bibliographical source for this book is the 'parent volume': *Ottoman Jerusalem. The Living City 1517-1917, Architectural survey by Yusuf Natsheh* (eds. Sylvia Auld and Robert Hillenbrand), 2 parts, London, 2000.

See also:

Abells, Z   *Jerusalem's water supply from the 18th century BCE to the present.* Jerusalem 1993

Ars Orientalis

Aron, A   'The Quarters of Jerusalem in the Ottoman Period', *Middle Eastern Studies* 28, 1992: 1-65

Arnold, T W   'Kadam Sharif' in *Encyclopédie de l'Islam*², 4. Leiden 1978: 383-4 (=*Encyclopaedia of Islam*², 4:-367-8)

'Asalī, al-, K J   'Jerusalem under the Ottomans AD 1516-1831' in (ed.) K J al-'Asali, *Jerusalem in History.* London 1989: 200-37

Atıl, E   *The Age of Süleyman the Magnificent.* New York 1987

Auld, S   'The Jewelled Surface: Architectural decoration of Jerusalem in the age of Süleyman-Qanuni' in (ed.) B Kühnel, *The Real and Ideal Jerusalem in Jewish, Christian and Islamic Art.* Jerusalem 1999: 467-79

Basha, el-, H   'Ottoman pictures of the Mosque of the Prophet in Madina as historical and documentary sources', *Islamic Art* 3, 1989: 227-33

Bates, Ü Ü   'A Study of Ottoman Period Architecture in Cairo 1517-1789' in (eds.) K-Kreiser, H-G Majer, M Restle and J Zick-Nissen, *Ars Turcica: Akten des VI. Internationalen Kongresses für Türkische Kunst.* 1987: 155-64

Bates, Ü Ü   'Two Ottoman Documents on Architects in Egypt', *Muqarnas* 3, 1985: 121-27

Behrens-Abouseif, D   *Egypt's Adjustment to Ottoman Rule. Institutions, Waqf and Architecture (16th and 17th centuries) in Cairo.* Leiden 1994

Behrens-Abouseif, D   'Sabils', in *Encyclopaedia of Islam*² 8, Leiden 1995: 679-83

Ben-Arieh, Y   *Jerusalem in the 19th Century—The Old City.* Jerusalem 1984

Bulletin d'études orientales

Berchem, M van   *Matériaux pour un corpus inscriptionum arabicarum.* Part II: Syrie du Sud—I. Jérusalem 'Ville'. Cairo 1920-23.

Berchem, M van   *Matériaux pour un corpus inscriptionum arabicarum.* Part II:—Syrie du Sud—II. Jérusalem 'Haram'. Cairo 1927

Bernus-Taylor, M (ed.)   *Soliman le Magnifique.* Paris 1990

Bieberstein, K and Bloedhorn, H   *Jerusalem. Grundzüge der Baugeschichte von Chalkolithikum bis zur Frühzeit der osmanischer Herrschaft*, 3 vols. Wiesbaden 1994

Bieberstein, K and Burgoyne, M H   *Tübinger Atlas des Vorderen Orients* B IV 7. Tübingen 1992

Broschi, M   'The inhabitants of Jerusalem' in N Rosovosky (ed.), *City of the Great King. Jerusalem from David to the Present.* Cambridge, Mass. 1996: 9-34

Burgoyne, M H   *A Chronological Index to Muslim Monuments of Jerusalem. Architecture of Islamic Jerusalem.* Jerusalem 1976

Burgoyne, M H   *Mamluk Jerusalem: An Architectural Study.* London 1987

Busse, H   'Die arabischen Inschriften im und am Felsendom in Jerusalem' in *Das Heilige Land* 109, 1-2, 1977: 8-24

Canaan, T   'The Palestinian Arab House: its architecture and folklore', *JPOS* 12, 1932: 223-47; 13, 1933: 1-83

Cengiz, O   'Khasseki', in *Encyclopaedia of Islam*², 4. Leiden 1978: 1100

Cerasi, M   'Late Ottoman Architects and Master Builders' *Muqarnas* 5, 1988: 77-102

Cohen, A   'Local Trade, International Trade and Government involvement in Jerusalem during the early Ottoman period', *Asian and African Studies* XII, 1978: 5-12

Cohen, A (ed.)   *History of Jerusalem in the beginning of the Ottoman Period.* Jerusalem 1981

Cohen, A   *Economic Life in Ottoman Jerusalem.* Cambridge 1989

Cohen, A   'The Walls of Jerusalem' in (eds.) C E Bosworth and others, *The Islamic World from Classical to Modern Times. Essays in honor of Bernard Lewis*, Princeton 1989: 467-77

Crane, H   *Risale-i Mi'mariyye: an Early Seventeenth-Century Ottoman Treatise on Architecture.* Leiden 1987

Crecelius, D   'The Waqf of Muḥammad Bey Abū al-Dhahab in Historical Perspective', *IJMES* 23, 1991: 57-81

Dalman, G   *Arbeit und Sitte in Palästina.* Leipzig and Hildesheim 1927-41

Denny, W *The Ceramics of the Mosque of Rüstem Pasha and the Environment of Change.* New York and London 1977

Denny, W 'Ceramic revetments of the Mosque of Rüstem Pasha' in (ed.) G Fehér, *Fifth International Congress of Turkish Art.* Budapest 1979: 269-91

Divine, D R *Politics and Society in Ottoman Palestine.* Colorado 1994

Doumani, B 'Palestinian Islamic Court Records: A source for socio-economic history', *MESA Bulletin* 19, 1985: 155-72

Dow, M *The Islamic Baths of Palestine.* Oxford 1996

Duda, D *Innenarchitektur syrischer Stadthäuser des 16. bis 18. Jahrhunderts.* Wiesbaden/Beirut 1971

Elad, A *Medieval Jerusalem and Islamic Worship. Holy Places, Ceremonies, Pilgrimage.* Leiden 1995

Erdmann, K 'Ka'bah-Fliesen', *AO* 3, 1959: 192-7

Esin, E 'Un manuscrit illustré représentant les sanctuaires de la Mècque et Médine et le Dôme du Mi'raj à l'époque des sultans turcs Sélim et Sülayman Ier (H.922-74/1516-66)', *Revue d'Histoire Maghrébine* 31-2, 1983: 409-10.

Faroqhi, S *Pilgrims and Sultans—The Hajj under the Ottomans 1517-1683.* London 1994

Gautier-van Berchem, M and Ory, S *Muslim Jerusalem in the work of Max van Berchem.* Geneva 1982

Gavin, C *The Image of the East: Nineteenth-Century Near Eastern Photographs by Bonfils.* Chicago 1982

Geva, H 'Excavations at the Citadel of Jerusalem 1976-1980' in (ed.) H Geva, *Ancient Jerusalem Revealed.* Jerusalem 1994: 156-67

Gilbar, G G (ed.) *Ottoman Palestine.* Leiden 1990

Goitein, S O 'Al-Kuds, A. History' in *Encyclopaedia of Islam*[2], 5, Leiden 1986: 322-39

Goodwin, G *A History of Ottoman Architecture.* London 1971

Goodwin, G 'The tekke of Süleyman I, Damascus', *PEQ* 110, 1978: 127-9

Göyünç, N 'The Procurement of Labor and Materials in the Ottoman Empire (16th and 18th centuries)' in (eds.) J-L Bacqué-Grammont and P Dumont, *Colloques Internationaux du Centre National de la Recherche Scientifique*, n.601. *Économie et Sociétés dans l' Empire Ottomane (fin du XVIIIe-début du XXe siècle).* Actes du colloque de Strasbourg, 1983: 327-33

Grotzfeld, H *Das Bad im arabisch-islamischen Mittelalter.* Wiesbaden 1962

Günsel, R 'Wall-paintings in Turkish Houses' in G Fehér (ed.) 5th *International Congress of Turkish Art.* Budapest 1978: 711-31

Hamilton, R W *The Structural History of the Aqsa Mosque.* London 1949

Hanna, N *Construction Work in Ottoman Cairo (1517-1798).* Cairo 1984

Harawi, al-, 'Alī ibn Abi Bakr (trans. J Sourdel-Thomine) *Guide des Lieux de Pélerinage.* Damascus 1957

Hasan, P 'The footprint of the Prophet', *Muqarnas* X (Essays in Honor of Oleg Grabar, contributed by his students). Leiden 1993: 335-43

Heyd, U *Ottoman Documents on Palestine 1552-1615. A study of the Firman according to the Mühimme Defteri.* Oxford 1960

Hillenbrand, R 'Das Vermächtnis des Felsendoms', in *Forschungsforum. Berichte aus der Otto-Friedrich-Universität* 2. Bamberg 1990: 64-71

Hütteroth, W-D and Abdulfattah, K *Historical Geography of Palestine, Transjordan and Southern Syria in the late 16th century.* Erlangen 1977

International Journal of Middle Eastern Studies

Inalcik, H and Lowry, H-W *Sultan Süleyman the Magnificent and his Times.* Washington DC and Chicago 1988

Ipṣīrlī, M 'The waqfs of Palestine in the sixteenth century according to the Tahrir register', in *The Third International Conference on Bilad al-Sham: Palestine April 1980*, 2. Amman 1984: 95-107

Johns, C N 'Guide to the Citadel of Jerusalem' *QDAP* 5, 1936: 127-31

Johns, C N *Guide to the Citadel of Jerusalem.* Publication of the Government of Palestine, Department of Antiquities. Jerusalem 1944

Johns, C N 'The Citadel, Jerusalem: A Summary of Work since 1934', *QDAP* 14 1950: 121-90

Jong, F de 'The Sufi Orders in Nineteenth and Twentieth-Century Palestine', *Studia Islamica* 48, 1983: 149-81

Journal of the Palestine Oriental Society

Journal of the Royal Asiatic Society

Journal of Semitic Studies

Kahle, P 'Gebräuche bei den moslemischen Heiligtümern in Palästina', *Palästinajahrbuch* 8, 1913: 139-78

Kappert, P *Geschichte Sultan Süleymān Ḳānūnīs von 1520 bis 1557, oder Ṭabaḳāt ül-memālik ve derecāt ül-mesālik von Celālzāde Muṣṭafā.* Wiesbaden 1981

Kunst des Orients

Kreiser, K 'Paschas und Scheiche. Mevlevî-Konvente in den grossen Städten des islamischen Ostens "nach Evliya Çelebi und anderen auch"', *Istanbul und das Osmanische Reich. Derwischwesen, Baugeschichte, Inscriftenkunde.* Istanbul 1995: 263-73

Kroyanker, D *Jerusalem Architecture—The Old City.* Jerusalem 1983

Kushner, D (ed.) *Palestine in the Late Ottoman Period: Political, Social and Economic Transformation.* Jerusalem and Leiden 1986

Lawless, R I 'The future of Historic Centres. Conservation or redevelopment' in (eds.) G H Blake and R I Lawless, *The Changing Middle Eastern City.* London and New York 1980: 178-208

Le Strange, G 'Description of the Noble Sanctuary at Jerusalem in 1470 AD by Kamal or Shams al-Din as-Suyuti', *JRAS* 19, 1887: 247-305

Le Strange, G *Palestine under the Moslems 650-1500.* Beirut 1965 (reprint of London edition, 1890)

Little, D P *A Catalogue of the Islamic Documents from al-Ḥaram al-Sharīf* in Jerusalem. *Beiruter Texte und Studien* 29. Wiesbaden and Beirut 1984

Little, D-P and Üner Turgay, A   'Documents from the Ottoman Period in the Khālidī Library in Jerusalem', *Die Welt des Islams* 20, 1980: 44-72

Lutfi, H   *Al-Quds al-Mamlukiyya: A History of Mamluk Jerusalem based on Haram documents, Islamkundliche Untersuchungen*, Band 113. Berlin 1985

Lybyer, A H   *The Government of the Ottoman Empire in the time of Suleiman the Magnificent.* New York 1966

Mandaville, J E   'The Jerusalem Shari'a Court Records: a Supplement and Complement of the Central Ottoman Archives' in (ed.) M Ma'oz, *Studies on Palestine during the Ottoman Period.* Jerusalem 1975: 517-24

Mandaville, J E   '"Usurious Piety": The Cash *Waqf* Controversy in the Ottoman Empire', *IJMES* 10, 1978: 289-308

Mantran, R and Sauvaget, J   *Règlements fiscaux Ottomans, Les Provinces Syriennes.* Damascus 1951

Ma'oz, M   *Palestine during the Ottoman period. Documents from Archives and Collections in Israel.* Jerusalem 1970

Ma'oz, M (ed.)   *Studies on Palestine during the Ottoman period.* Jerusalem 1975

Marcus, A   *The Middle East on the Eve of Modernity: Aleppo in the Eighteenth Century.* New York 1989

Matson, G   *The Middle East in Pictures.* New York 1980

Mayer, L A   'The Inspector of Building in the Mamluk period', *Bulletin of the Institute of Jewish Studies of Hebrew University* 1, 1925: 87-91

Megaw, A H S   *Qubbat as Sakhra (The Dome of the Rock). An account of the building and its condition with recommendations for its conservation, submitted to the Supreme Moslem Council* (revised). Jerusalem (typescript) 1952

Meinecke, M   'Die Architektur des 16. Jahrhunderts in Kairo, nach der Osmanischen Eroberung von 1517', *IVème Congrés International d'Art Turc 1971,* Aix-en-Provence and Paris 1976: 145-52

Meinecke, M   'Die osmanische Architektur des 16. Jahrhunderts in Damaskus', in (ed.) G. Fehér, *Fifth International Congress of Turkish Art.* Budapest 1978: 575-85

Meinecke, M   *The Restoration of al-Quds, Jerusalem by the Ottoman Sultan Sulayman Qanuni.* Damascus 1987

Meinecke, M   *Die Mamlukische Architektur in Ägypten und Syrien 648/1250 bis 923/1517,* Abhandlungen des Deutschen Archäologischen Instituts Kairo. Islamische Reihe. Band 5. Glückstadt 1992

Middle East Studies Association Bulletin

Milstein, R   'Drawings of the Haram of Jerusalem in Ottoman Manuscripts', in (eds.) A Singer, A Cohen, *Aspects of Ottoman History, Papers from CIÉPO 9, Scripta Hierosolymitana XXV.* Jerusalem 1994: 62-9

Milstein, R   *King Solomon's Seal.* Jerusalem 1995: 175-79

Mitchell, H G   'The Modern Wall of Jerusalem', *Annual of the American School of Oriental Research in Jerusalem* I, 1920: 28-50

Mitteilungen des deutschen archäologischen Instituts

Mostafa, S L   'The Cairene Sabil: Form and Meaning', *Muqarnas* 6, 1990: 33-42

Mujir al-Din, al-Ulaimi al-Hanbali, 'Abd al-Rahman ibn Muhammad   *Al-uns al-jalīl fī tārīkh al-Quds wa'l-Khalīl.* Amman 1973. (Trans.) H Sauvaire, *Histoire de Jérusalem et d'Hébron … Fragments de la Chronique de Moudjir-ed-dyn.* Paris 1876

Necipoğlu, G   'Süleyman the Magnificent and the representation of power in the context of Ottoman-Hapsburg-Papal rivalry', *The Art Bulletin* 81/3, 1989: 401-27

Necipoğlu, G   'From International Timurid to Ottoman: A Change in Taste in Sixteenth-Century Ceramic Tiles', *Muqarnas* 7, 1990: 136-70

Neuwirth, A   'The Spiritual Meaning of Jerusalem in Islam', in (ed.) N Rosovsky, *Jerusalem—City of David.* Cambridge, Mass. and London 1996: 93-116

Nir, Y   *The Bible and the Image. The History of Photography in the Holy Land 1839-1899.* Philadelphia 1985

Ôgel, S   'Die Innenfläche der osmanischen Kuppel', *Anatolica* 5, 1973-6: 219-33

Onne, E   *Photographic Heritage of the Holy Land, 1839-1914.* Manchester 1980

Otto-Dorn, K   'Osmanischen ornamentale Wandmalerei', *K des O* I, 1950: 45-54

Pascual, J P   *Damas à la fin du XVI siècle d'après trois waqfs ottomans,* Institut Français de Damas. Damascus 1983

Palestine Exploration Fund Quarterly

Peri, O   'The Waqf as an instrument to increase and consolidate political power; the case of Khasseki Sultan Waqf in the late Eighteenth Century' in (eds.) G R Warburg and G G Gilbar, *Studies in Islamic Society—Contributions in Memory of Gabriel Baer.* Haifa 1984: 47-62

Peters, F E   *Jerusalem. The Holy City in the eyes of chroniclers, visitors, pilgrims and prophets from the days of Abraham to the beginnings of modern times.* Princeton 1985

Peters, F E   *Jerusalem and Mecca: The typology of the Holy City in the Near East.* New York 1986

Peters, F E   *Distant Shrine: The Islamic centuries in Jerusalem.* AMS Studies in Modern Society; Political and Social Issues, 22. New York 1993

Petersen, A   'Early Ottoman Forts on the Darb al-Hajj', *Levant* 21, 1989: 97-117

Prag, K   *Jerusalem. Blue Guide.* London and New York 1989

Quarterly of the Department of Antiquities of Palestine

Rafeq, A K   *The Province of Damascus 1723-83.* Beirut 1966

Rafeq, A K   'The law-court registers of Damascus with special reference to craft-corporations during the first half of the eighteenth century', *Les arabes par leurs archives (XVIe-XXe siècles),* 1976: 141-59

Rafeq, A K   'The Syrian 'Ulama', Ottoman Law and Islamic

Shari'a', *Turcica, Revue d'Études Turques* 26, 1994: 9-32

Raymond, A 'Le sultan Süleymân et l'activité architecturale dans les provinces arabes de l'Empire 1520-1566' in (ed.) G Veinstein, *Soliman le Magnifique et son temps.* Paris 1992: 371-84

Raymond, A *The Great Islamic Cities in the 16-18th centuries: an Introduction.* London and New York 1984

Richmond, E T *The Dome of the Rock in Jerusalem. A Description of its Structure and Decoration.* Oxford 1924

Rihawi, A and Ouéchek, E E 'Les deux *takiyya* de Damas. La *takiyya* et la *madrasa* Sulaymaniyya du Marj et la *takiyya* as-Salimiyya de Salihiyya', *BEO* 28, 1975: 217-25

Rogers, J M '*Waqfiyyas* and *Waqaf*-registers. New primary sources for Islamic architecture', *K des O* 12, 1976-7: 182-96

Rogers, J M 'The State and the Arts in Ottoman Turkey. Part II: the furnishing and decoration of Süleymaniye', *IJMES* 14/3, 1982: 283-313

Rogers, J M and Ward, R M *Süleyman the Magnificent.* London 1988

Rosen-Ayalon, M 'On Suleiman's sabils in Jerusalem' in (eds.) C E Bosworth and others, *The Islamic World: From Classical to Modern Times. Essays in honor of Bernard Lewis.* Princeton 1989: 589-607

Sack, D *Damaskus. Entwicklung und Struktur einer orientalischen islamischen Stadt.* Mainz-am-Rhein 1989

St Laurent, B and Riedlmayer, A 'Restorations of Jerusalem and the Dome of the Rock and Their Political Significance 1537-1928', *Muqarnas* 10, 1992: 76-84

Salam-Liebich, H *The Architecture of the Mamluk City of Tripoli.* Cambridge, Mass. 1983

Schick, C 'Die Baugeschichte der Stadt Jerusalem', *ZDPV* 17, 1894-95: 261-76

Schiller, E (ed.) *The first photographs of Jerusalem.* Jerusalem 1978

Schiller, E *Jerusalem and the Holy Land in Old Engravings and Illustrations 1483-1800.* Jerusalem 1981

Sharon, M 'The political role of the bedouins in Palestine in the sixteenth and seventeenth centuries', in (ed.) M Ma'oz, *Studies on Palestine during the Ottoman Period.* Jerusalem 1975: 11-30

Singer, A *Palestinian peasants and Ottoman officials: Rural administration around sixteenth-century Jerusalem.* Cambridge 1994

Siriyya, E 'The Journeys of 'Abd al-Ghani al-Nabulsi in Palestine (1101/1690 and 1105/1693)', *JSS* 24/1, 1979: 55-69

Skilliter, S A 'Khurrem', in *Encyclopaedia of Islam*[2], 5. Leiden 1986: 66-7

Stephan, St H 'Two Turkish inscriptions from the Citadel of Jerusalem', *QDAP* 2, 1933: 132-5

Stephan, St H (with notes by L A Mayer) 'Evliya Tshelebi's Travels in Palestine', *QDAP* 4 (1935), 103-8, 154-7; 5 (1936), 69-73; 6 (1938), 84-97; 8 (1939), 137-56;

9 (1939), 81-104

Stephan, St H 'An Endowment Deed of Khasseki Sultan dated 24th May 1552', *QDAP* 10, 1940: 170-99

Stephan, St H *Evliya Tschelebi's Travels in Palestine 1648-1650.* Complete works of Evliya Tschelebi reprinted from *QDAP* 4-9, 1935-49. Jerusalem 1980

Tabbaa, Y 'Sabil and Shadirwan in Medieval Islamic Courtyards', *Environmental Design* I, 1986: 34-7

Tell, al-, S K 'The exterior tile decoration of the Dome of the Rock in Jerusalem', in *First International Congress on Turkish Tiles and Ceramics. Communications program 6-11.VII.1986.* Kütahya 1989: 15-24

Tibawi, A-L *The Islamic Pious Foundations in Jerusalem.* London 1978

Vogt-Göknil, O *Living Architecture: Ottoman.* London 1966

Wahrman, D 'Developing a Photographic Milieu' in *Capturing the Holy Land: MJ Diness and the Beginnings of Photography in Jerusalem.* Harvard 1993

Walls, A G 'Ottoman restorations to the Sabil and to the Madrasa of Qaytbay in Jerusalem', *Muqarnas* 10, 1993: 85-97

Walls, A G and Abu'l-Hajj, A *Arabic Inscriptions in Jerusalem: A Handlist and Maps.* London 1980

Watzinger, C and Wulzinger, K *Damaskus. Die islamische Stadt.* Berlin 1924

Wightman, G J *The Walls of Jerusalem, from the Canaanites to the Mamluks.* Mediterranean Archaeology Supplement 4. Sydney 1993

Wilkinson, J D 'The Streets of Jerusalem', *Levant* 7, 1975: 118-36

Williams, J A 'The Monuments of Ottoman Cairo', *Colloque internationale sur l'histoire du Caire.* Gräfenhainichen 1972: 453-63

Wilson, C W 'The Masonry of the Haram Wall', *PEFQS* 1880: 9-65

Wirth, H 'Die Beziehungen der orientalisch–islamischen Stadt zum umgebenden Lande. Ein Beitrag zur Theorie des Rentenkapitalismus' in (ed.) E Meynen, *Geographie heute. Einheit und Vielfalt. Ernst Plewe zu seinem 65 Geburtstag.* Wiesbaden 1973: 323-33

Yenişehirlioğlu, F (ed.) *Ottoman Architecture: works outside Turkey—Türkiye disindaki Osmanli mimari yapitari.* Ankara 1989

Yenişehirlioğlu, F 'Tile Samples from the Dome of the Rock and their Twentieth-Century Reproductions', in (ed.) T Majda, *Seventh International Congress of Turkish Art.* Warsaw 1991

Zeitschrift des deutschen Palästina-Vereins

Ze'evi, D 'The Sufi Connection: Jerusalem Notables in the Seventeenth Century' in (eds.) A Singer and A Cohen, *Aspects of Ottoman History: Papers from CIÉPO 9, Jerusalem.* Jerusalem 1994: 126-42

Ze'evi, D *An Ottoman Century. The District of Jerusalem in the 1660s.* Albany, NY 1996

INDEX

OTTOMAN JERUSALEM
THE LIVING CITY 1517-1917

Edited by
SYLVIA AULD and ROBERT HILLENBRAND
Architectural survey by YUSUF NATSHEH

The Ottoman empire dominated the Mediterranean and the Middle East from the 16th to the 18th centuries until the Europeans began to assert power in the region. However, the Ottomans continued to control much of the region until after their defeat in the First World War.

Within the land of Palestine, the city of Jerusalem occupied a special position. The Ottomans inherited a city which for Muslims featured the exceptional presence of the Dome of the Rock and the rich inheritance of buildings from the Mamluk period. However, for visitors today much of the aspect of the Old City, dominated by its magnificent walls, is that created during this period of Ottoman rule.

This extensive and detailed work presents for the first time a wide-ranging study of various facets of the Ottoman city. A wealth of socio-historical research is supplemented by an important architectural survey. Under the direction of Professor Robert Hillenbrand, a team of internationally acknowledged academics and specialists have produced an erudite corpus of material which will serve as a standard work on the subject for the foreseeable future and which will serve as a superb complementary volume to WIFT's acclaimed *Mamluk Jerusalem*: a further four centuries of the Holy City's Islamic heritage.

Contributors

Robert Hillenbrand
Abdul-Karim Rafeq
Khairiah Kasmieh
Klaus Kreiser
Martin Strohmeier
Ernst Axel Knauf
Angelika Neuwirth
Michele Bernardini
Khadr Salameh

Mohammad 'Ali 'Alami
Mahmud Atallah
Lawrence I Conrad
Paolo Cuneo
Rashid I Khalidi
George Hintlian
Ruth Victor Hummel
Kamal J al-'Asali

Nancy Micklewright
Claudia Ott
Vera Tamari
Sylvia Auld
Susan Roaf
Beatrice St Laurent
John Carswell
Finbarr B Flood

James W Allan
Marwan Abu Khalaf
Sharif M Sharif
Michael Hamilton Burgoyne
Mahmud Hawari
Martin Dow
David M Myres
Yusuf Natsheh

298 x 220 mm, over 1,200 pages in two parts with 16 pages in full colour, over 500 plans, drawings, black and white photographs, both parts fully bound within a slip case.
£145.00
ISBN 1 901435 03 2

Altajir World of Islam Trust
11 Elvaston Place, London SW7 5QG, England